First Print Edition 2024.

Aude Publishing

Introduction

In this book, we introduce you to the Ethereum cryptocurrency network and take a dive into the many common questions that are asked about how Ethereum works, what investing in Ethereum looks like, and what some common concerns are about cryptocurrency in general.

By the end of the book, you will be able to understand the core principles of operation that enable Ethereum to reach the heights that it has. Ethereum is a powerful platform that holds great promise for the future of decentralized financial systems that are still in their infancy. The future is bright with the promise new financial systems and concepts can be tried and tested without the bureaucracy of centralized systems. Ethereum is not perfect, but the governance is continuously seeking to improve its capabilities, and you will learn here the pros and cons of this unique and pioneering cryptocurrency platform.

What is Ethereum?

Ethereum is an open-source, blockchain based technology platform. Ethereum consists of a network of over 2,900 computers working together to store and maintain a transaction ledger at a rate of up to 30 transactions per second. In this traditional cryptocurrency realm, Ethereum is similar to Bitcoin and other well-known blockchain base currencies. At its core, Ethereum is a purely virtual means to create and store financial value. These types of technology enable privacy, anonymity, and transparency in the world of virtual finance. More than this, Ethereum is a platform that enables hundreds of thousands of independent cryptocurrency ecosystems that run on top of it. Called 'tokens', these independent objects can be bought, sold, generated, burned, and transferred using the same Ethereum platform. Ethereum also adds the concept of 'smart contracts' which can power a multitude of intelligent capabilities, for both the core Ethereum currency and the token ecosystems.

Ethereum is multi-dimensional in a way that is

unique to cryptocurrency. Due to its complexity, individuals can be overwhelmed by the concepts and possibilities. As such, in drilling down in this book with specific, targeted questions and thorough answers, you can come away with a better understanding of this powerful platform. With a fairly basic understanding, you could create your own token ecosystem on the platform that goes viral and brings economic independence to thousands of people. Or, you may use the information to audit and carefully scrutinize existing tokens or Decentralized Finance (DeFi) projects before investing, thus safeguarding your money. Either way, Ethereum is truly a fascinating world within cryptocurrency.

Who Started Ethereum?

The concept of the Ethereum platform was first put forward by Vitalik Buterin, in 2013. Buterin is a Russian-Canadian programmer who introduced the conceptual framework for what would become Ethereum his whitepaper. Through 2014, Buterin worked with a group of individuals to form what is today known as the Ethereum Foundation. Development was crowdfunded, with investors purchasing Ether (ETH) with Bitcoin (BTC) in order to get the project off the ground.

Buterin's involvement with cryptocurrency began in 2011, when he started writing for *Bitcoin Weekly*, and later for *Bitcoin Magazine* of which he was a co-founder. His involvement in the Bitcoin community helped to ground him firmly in the concept of cryptocurrency and inspire him toward what he viewed as a next generation opportunity.

While Ethereum was started more as a public and transparent organization, Buterin's involvement with the project has given him something of a figurehead status, and his opinions and activities hold some sway over the financial performance of the network and underlying tokens.

Since Ethereum's inception, the Ethereum Foundation has driven the technical development of the network. At the beginning, Ethereum was functionally just another cryptocurrency that had the added state-machine capability. With the Foundation's process of adding new capabilities to the network, Vitalik Buterin and the team have brought forward now-ubiquitous features such as token side-chains, sharding, NFT capabilities, and more.

How Does Ethereum Work?

Ethereum is a cryptocurrency that consists of wallets, a currency (Ether), blocks, nodes, and miners. Each block that is produced contains the record of transactions made; the blocks are stored on the nodes, and created by the miners. On top of all this rides a programmable platform, the Ethereum Virtual Machine (EVM) that takes the classic distributed ledger capability of cryptocurrency and transforms it into a massively distributed state machine. This means that programmable computer code can be executed by the thousands of Ethereum clients active at any one time. Each block on the chain not only stores transactions in the standard sense, but also the 'state' of this virtual machine. Most commonly the 'smart contract' functionality allows the network to intelligently create and perform transactions based on pre-defined programming. While traditional cryptocurrencies require an endpoint (node or client) to generate transactions, the EVM allows programmed functions to be stored and executed by the network as a whole. In this way, there is consensus regarding the intelligent functions that are being run.

As an example, the following is possible with a smart contract function:

1) Create a token with a maximum supply of 1,000,000 tokens.

2) Distribute the token evenly to 100,000 wallets (10 tokens per wallet).

3) On every transaction, send 0.5% of the value to a 'burn' address and distribute 0.5% of the transaction to all current holders of the token.

These types of rules are only possible with the distributed computing that Ethereum enables and would simply not be possible from a classic ledger-type cryptocurrency.

From its inception, Ethereum has functioned around the Proof-of-Work (PoW) mechanism for processing of blocks and rewarding participation in the network. Mining systems compete to produce the next block in the network which will contain all of the current transactions. The network adjusts difficulty to allow the mining workstations to produce a new block roughly every twelve seconds. If more systems begin mining, the difficulty will increase in order to maintain this desired timeframe. The winning miner will have around 2 ETH credited to their wallet, and will also be reimbursed for gas fees incurred by the transactions included in the block.

With the eventual advent of Eth 2.0, the Ethereum network will move to a Proof-of-Stake model, in which expensive and power-hungry mining systems will no longer be needed. Instead, those wishing to participate in the network must stake (deposit) an amount of ETH in order to become a 'validator'. Validator nodes will perform the same function as the mining system. The network will randomly select a validator to produce a given block, while the other validator nodes not selected will confirm the block. The chosen validator will receive the reward for that block. The new PoS model also allows for a technique known as 'sharding', which implements multiple chains on the network. Multiple chains can be operated simultaneously and push the transaction-per-second power of the entire network into the hundreds of thousands.

What is the history of Ethereum?

Ethereum was first described in 2013 by Vitalik Buterin. The core principles and concepts were worked out between Buterin and seven other founders through 2015. After several prototype platforms were tested by beta testers, on July 30th, 2015, the 'Genesis' block was mined and the blockchain in use today was born.

A major split in the Ethereum network occurred in 2016, after the 'DAO' event where hackers stole a large amount of ether from a new Decentalized Autonomous Organization. In order to overcome the issue, the Ethereum foundation reverted the blockchain in a way that allowed the funds to be returned to the DAO investors. Network nodes whose operators chose not to participate in the reversion formed the Ethereum Classic network, which is still in operation.

Several hard forks over time have introduced new reward structures and features through the Ethereum Improvement Proposal (EIP) process, such as NFT capabilities and automatic burning. Many of the updates are in support of the ETH 2.0 goal which will increase transaction throughput through a mechanism called 'sharding', which involves running many blockchains in parallel. ETH 2.0 will also fully incorporate the Proof-of-Stake (PoS) consensus mechanism. This new consensus mechanism will greatly reduce the environmental impact of Ethereum, which makes is largely more favorable as a platform. Most of these updates are expected to take place in 2022.

How popular is Ethereum?

Ethereum is the second most popular cryptocurrency by market cap and third most popular by trading volume, following Tether (USDT) and Bitcoin (BTC). With over 181 million addresses on the Ethereum blockchain, and some 868,000 active addresses, Ethereum is at least as popular as Bitcoin in terms of active accounts, according to BitInfoCharts.com. Crucially, active addresses do not necessarily include people holding Ethereum since their accounts may not show any activity.

What is the point of Ethereum?

Ethereum is designed to be a cryptocurrency platform that enabled a new generation of web-enabled decentralized finance applications. It does this through the use of smart contracts, which are scripts that operate autonomously as the blockchain processes data and transactions. Ethereum was conceived as a complete platform for supporting an almost unlimited number of financial applications that don't require traditional banking infrastructure at all.

Is Ethereum Secure?

Yes, Ethereum is generally considered to be secure. Cryptographically, the core wallet system that uses private keys / public keys / public addresses is highly secure. There are potential security risks in applications that interact with your wallet. If a website or exchange where you may store Ether gets hacked, it is possible to lose them. For this reason it is generally advised to store Ether in a hardware wallet or other secure non-cloud location, with a backup of your keys securely stored.

Because Ethereum has the added programmability, there is also a possibility of scam contracts being implemented on the platform that can be used for malicious purposes. Many reputable distributed finance groups are now having their contracts audited in order to provide peace of mind to their users; but it is possible for other contract creators to create contracts that could drain your wallet of funds. Therefore it is wise to be extremely cautious when interacting with any website or function that asks for permission to interact with your wallet.

Will Ethereum Run Out?

Ethereum was designed to have no end to its emission, so it will not run out. One side effect of this perpetual emission model is inflation; but new rules and fee/burning mechanism that have been recently implemented will combat the inflationary pressure. It is possible that the burn rate could exceed the emission rate for a period of time, and it is also possible that users could hoard Ethereum, making it more scarce, but not unobtainable.

Is Ethereum a company?

As Ethereum was developed, a non-profit foundation called the 'Ethereum Foundation' was formed to administer the Initial Coin Offering (ICO) and support the development of the software. As such, Ethereum is governed by a non-profit foundation as opposed to a commercial entity.

What are Ethereum addresses?

Ethereum addresses define a wallet. Ethereum addresses start out as a string of 64 hexadecimal characters which define the 'private key'. The private key should only be ever known to the owner of the wallet. The private key gives automatic and instant access to any funds stored in the wallet.

From the private key, a special cryptographic function called a Elliptic Curve Digital Signature Algorithm (ECDSA) is applied and hashed. The last twenty bytes of this hashed output is the public address of the wallet; adding 0x to the beginning of the public address provides the standard Ethereum address that can be used to receive funds. The public address serves strictly as an identifier, and does not provide any access to funds received. Multiple addresses can be associated to an account, allowing for multiple streams of funds to be received into a wallet for different purposes.

What is an Ethereum node?

An Ethereum node is a computer system that runs Ethereum client software. The software downloads, stores, and shares the part of rall of the Ethereum blockchain to other clients. In the Ethereum ecosystem, there are actually three different types of nodes that can be run. Running an Ethereum node local to your own Ethereum-interfaces applications can be highly beneficial in terms of ensuring the lowest possible latency for transactions. Because the node is being run locally, you can trust that it is secure and you don't necessarily need to trust a third party node. You can also choose to ensure redundancy against things like hardware failures or power outages, knowing in full how your system is configured. This is not possible with a third party node that may go offline unexpectedly.

Who are Ethereum miners?

Ethereum miners are individuals who contribute computing power to the network. Miners can either mine individually or through a pool that aggregates the computing power to the network, and then divides the rewards proportionally. Mining pools can be highly complex and decentralized, even to having their own apps and mining tools (such as Nicehash), or they can be privately run amongst a group of friends or partners. The successful miners, individually or in a pool, are rewarded by the network with the new currency emitted with each new block, along with transaction fees according to the network rules.

What is an Ethereum wallet?

An Ethereum wallet represents one or more keypairs (private key / public key) that collates and presents the available funds and transaction options to the wallet owner. A user accesses the wallet either through a local client program or a web wallet. Any wallet program that has the right private key can access the funds associated with that wallet; so ownership of the wallet is really tied to the private key, which makes it highly important to protect the private key from unauthorized access.

What types of Ethereum wallets are there?

With Ethereum, as with many different cryptocurrencies, there are multiple ways to store the 'wallet', which is really just a private key that provides access to the funds.

Paper Wallet: A paper wallet ability created a printed document that stores the private key as a QR code or numerically for future use. Done correctly, this is likely one of the most secure methods for storing the private key associated with the wallet. The wallet can be generated offline, but most commonly is done online through a website such as MyEtherWallet. Once the wallet is generated, a keystore file is provided for download and printing. You do not need the paper wallet receive Ethereum, as long as you keep a copy of the public address handy for providing to other individuals. They will be able to send Ethereum to the public address, and you can monitor the balance of the paper wallet via a block explorer. Only when you yourself wish to send Ethereum, or trade it, do you need to pull out the paper wallet and import the private key to an online tool to begin making transactions.

Online Wallet: An online wallet is a web site or web app that stores your private key, or downloads it to your computer for use later. You can quickly see your balance and make transactions without needing to download the blockchain to your computer. This type of wallet may be inherently less secure, since you need to trust the online wallet operator and they may be hacked. One of the more popular online wallets includes Exodus Wallet, which supports a lot of cryptocurrencies and tokens in addition to Ethereum.

What is Ethereum versus Ether?

Ethereum is the term used to describe the network, platform, and overall ecosystem of the network. It is also the name of the Foundation that provides governorship and technical guidance of the network. Ether is the actual coin that is produced on the network, and used for transaction fees for any action that takes places on the network - including the sending of any tokens that are supported by the network.

What is Ethereum mining?

Mining, in cryptocurrency, is the process of a computer, graphics card, or Application Specific Integrated Circuit (ASIC) trying to discover the answer to a cryptocurrency's 'block'. Each miner competes in a race to find the answer with all of the other network's miners. Once the answer is found, that miner is allowed to generate the block and submit it to the network for verification and validation, which is done by the nodes. All Proof-of-Work based cryptocurrencies use some form of mining with a variety of mining algorithms to keep the blockchain moving forward. Ethereum uses the 'EthHash' mining algorithm. This particular algorithm is ASIC resistant, which means that ASICs cannot be easily developed to provide a mining advantage. Ethereum has a high memory requirement for mining, and is primarily mined used GPUs with 6 or more GB or vRAM.

Is Ethereum mining profitable?

Like many topics in cryptocurrency, the short answer is - it depends. Because mining is a competitive activity, the more hashing power you can bring to the competition, the more likely it will be that you will win blocks and reap rewards. As other miners contribute to the network, and the overall hash rate grows, your own contribution becomes smaller and the rewards may be smaller or less frequent. With the shift to Eth 2.0, which eliminated the mining mechanism from the Ethereum network, it is probably not profitable to get into mining Ethereum at this point, with the associated cost of hardware. Individuals with existing hardware suitable to mining Ethereum can probably continue to be profitable until the switch to Proof-of-Stake (PoS).

Are there real, physical Ether?

Ethereum, and it's concomitant currency Ether exist only virtually within the network. While there may be representations of Ether printed or made, either 3D printed, or cast, or moulded in some way, the actual currency is strictly digital and exist only within the blockchain network. One can purchase these physical representations of the currency in a variety of materials, though they do no represent any value with regard to the Ethereum wallet - and indeed, one could purchase these coins without any access to an Ethereum wallet. They would be completely decoupled from the network and blockchain.

Is Ethereum frictionless?

A frictionless financial system generally has a low barrier to performing transactions, e.g. fees and latencies are low enough so as to have a negligible impact on operations. Ethereum, with it's high gas fees and frequent transaction lag, is far from it. Other networks, such as Polygon, have tried to play off of that limitation of Ethereum and advertise themselves as being much closer to a frictionless platform.

With the advent of ETH 2.0, it is hoped that the greater scale for transactions and the resulting lower gas fees will also move this powerful platform closer to that ideal goal.

Does Ethereum use mnemonic phrases?

The ability to use mnemonic phrases as a backup access to a wallet is both a blessing and a curse. A mnemonic phrase is a list of words that, taken together, allow a wallet client to re-create an existing wallet address and provide access to it. It takes the places of a private key, which is a long hexadecimal string of letters and numbers that is hard to remember and easy to corrupt. A mnemonic phrase is a potential security risk, in that anyone with the list of words can recreate the wallet and claim any funds within it. It is easier, potentially, to brute force a word list instead of a long private key string.

Bitcoin Improvement Proposal 39 (BIP-39) first proposed the use of mnemonic phrases for easier recovery. Most wallets now support this same mechanism, and often provide the mnemonic phrase during the setup process. Ethereum is no different, and supports this capability as part of the wallet creation process.

Can you get Ethereum back if you send it to the wrong address?

Typically, once a cryptocurrency is sent to an address there is no way to recall it. If Ethereum is sent by mistake to the wrong address, and you are unable to communicate with the holder of that address (or worse, if nobody has control over the address) it would be considered lost or burned. With such a large number of addresses, the likelihood of a real person being on the receiving end of a typo'd address is actually very small, and the funds would need to be considered burned. If there's is, by chance, a person on the other end of the wrong transaction there is always the possibility they would return the funds if they were not expecting them.

How would you explain Ethereum to a 5-year-old?

Ethereum is computer money than you can send or receive from other people. You can also use the Ethereum computer money to make other money with any name you choose! You can buy or sell any of this money using your computer or phone, and use special numbers to send the money to other people. Very clever people can also write special computer programs using Ethereum to allow them to make their own money, and send it to other people.

Is Ethereum a scam?

While Ethereum itself is not a scam, and has governance from the Ethereum Foundation and a large and robust group of individuals that participate in the platform, it is possible for others to use Ethereum to run scams on unsuspecting investors. Here are a couple of examples of nefarious activities that have taken place:

* Users may find 'airdropped' tokens in their wallet that were placed there by the scammers. When a user goes to a decentralized exchange (DEX) to trade the tokens, they have to approve access to their wallet for that token. Without reviewing the 'contract', the sign off on it via their wallet. The permission they signed off on also allowed access to other coins or tokens in the wallet, which get traded away and stolen, leaving the user with worthless tokens.

* Initial Coin Offering (ICO) scams were more common in the earlier days of the token economy. This would involve a hyped up company doing interviews, having a top-quality website, and selling a token on the network. After the ICO is

over, the token becomes worthless, but the company that held the ICO has all of the Ether, Bitcoin, or other coins that were paid to them for the tokens. The SEC has since started pursuing and prosecuting such individuals.

* A 'rug pull' involves the release of a token, typically with some hype, on the platform. It trades on a DEX and becomes valuable. The originators of the token sell their holdings, and remove the liquidity that is required to allow trades to occur. This leaves the rest of the token participants holding the bag with no effective way to trade out of their position. This has become a more common scam, and requires careful consideration and research before taking a position in a token.

* DeFi Farming is a fairly new trend that involves staking tokens on a farm. The farm will reward stakeholders with some other token (usually branded with the Farm - such as KRILL or MOON) based on their stake size. Occasionally these farms are scams and the farm creators can make off with some or all of the staked tokens. Alternately, the farm may be hacked due to poor security practices on the part of the creators, and

some third party may make off with the tokens.

Don't be scammed. It pays to research and verify the validity of where you put your coins or tokens. Because there is so little regulation in the community, you really are on your own - especially when investing in some of the more pioneering aspects of the cryptocurrency world.

Can Ethereum be hacked?

Because Ethereum operates on an open and exposed blockchain, it is not so easy to hack. Possible attacks include 51% attacks, brute-force attacks against private keys, and hack attempts against centralized exchanges.

- Centralized Exchanges

Centralized exchanges have their own software, often developed in-house, that handles the high speed interactions needed to trade cryptocurrency effectively. These exchanges require you to deposit funds for trading, and those funds are very much within the control of the exchange, and in the exchange's own wallet. Because exchanges do not typically use any open-source software, there is not a robust auditing process around their networks or configurations. If there is a suitable cybersecurity weakness in the exchange platform, it is absolutely possible for theft to occur. Internal exchange employees, too, may have credentials that permit them to engage in theft. Exchange users with weak credentials, or credentials that have been leaked from other hacks, may also become victims of theft

- though such theft would be limited to a smaller group of individuals.

- Brute-force Attacks

Because most cryptocurrency wallets exist as a private-key/public-key pair, and because the process for generating the public key and wallet address from the private key is a known method, it is possible for clever hackers to brute-force a wallet with a balance and transfer those funds somewhere else. The main defense against this process is the sheer scope of private keys available to use, and the face that every wallet's private key is chosen at random (except in very specific cases). A private key is two hundred and fifty six bits long. Represented in hexademical, a private key looks like:

8da4ef21b864d2cc526dbdb2a120bd2874c36c9 d0a1fb7f8c63d7f7a8b41de8f

Each digit of the private key can represent sixteen different values (0-9, A-F). A brute force attack works off of a single or list of public addresses. The attack can be performed on a CPU or

GPU for higher speed. The brute force software generates private key values and runs them through the address generation process to see if they match. If a match is found, the private key is output to the screen or dumped to a file. If no match is found, the system continues searching. Modern processors can perform this function at over one million keys per second per core, while graphics processors can perform these functions at over two billion keys per second assuming the system is tuned properly. While this sounds like a lot, and may make one concerned over the security at the core of cryptocurrency, it is in practice not at all a threat. Because of the sheer number of possibilities (the number of private keys available is greater than atoms in the universe) it would take an absolutely impossible amount of time, statistically speaking, to find even one wallet - longer than the longest estimates of the age of the earth.

While this bodes very well for the security of cryptocurrency, it emphasizes the importance of retaining your wallet backups or mnenomic phrases. If lost, nobody can recover your wallet for you.

- 51% Attacks

A 51% attack is an attack upon the blockchain itself. Essentially, a group of miners with sufficient hash power are able to begin denying blocks from being confirmed and transactions from going through. Worse than this, they may effectively reverse transactions which can allow individuals to double-spend their currency. Attackers would be unable to modify existing blocks, but they can definitely wreak havoc on the chain on a go-forward basis. This type of attack on established blockchains would likely require substantial coordination and hashing capability. For new coins that have been recently introduced and where the network is still developing, it is possible for this type of attack to be highly effective and potentially destructive to an otherwise useful cryptocurrency.

Who keeps track of Ethereum transactions?

Ethereum is a decentralized blockchain, where any number of Ethereum network nodes are storing the blocks as the network produces them. As such, anyone who runs a node is helping to keep track of the transactions. On top of this, websites like https://etherscan.io provide a service called a 'Block Explorer' which is an easy-to-use front-end to allow anyone to see the transactions, wallet balances, tokens, and blocks at any point in time.

Some of the most popular block explorers are:

https://etherscan.io
https://etherchain.org
https://ethplorer.io
https://blockchair.com/ethereum

These services run on top of one or more node servers to parse and track all aspects of the blockchain historically through the present. They provide a valuable service to end users who may want to verify their transactions have gone through, for instance.

Can anyone buy and sell Ethereum?

Generally, yes! It is possible and fairly easy to buy or sell Ethereum using sites like Coinbase, which allow you to use fiat currency to purchase cryptocurrency. Typically, regulation requires anyone using these sites to register and provide government identification to verify their identity. This also helps when it comes time to cash out any cryptocurrencies, because the site will provide tax information to you and to the government. Because of this, it would be difficult for young people to purchase Ethereum directly.

Some governments have tried to ban cryptocurrency transactions in their countries. In these cases, it may be more difficult to access a site that would allow Ethereum to be purchased; but with the use of VPNs and other tools that can obfuscate one's location, it still can be done.

Is Ethereum Anonymous?

The core nature of Ethereum and other cryptocurrencies is inherently anonymous. In theory, a person can mine Ethereum, hold it, swap to various tokens within the Ethereum ecosystem, and swap back to Ethereum completely anonymously. The anonymity becomes more complex when working with services external to Ethereum, such as exchanges. Because of government regulation, almost all exchange services require registration and some form of identity verification in order to cash out. This aids the exchanges in compliance with tax law, as cashing out cryptocurrency typically requires some form of tax to be paid to the government. As such, Ethereum itself is anonymous, but interfacing with external resources with Ethereum is typically not anonymous.

Can the rules of Ethereum change?

The Ethereum network has many rules and protocols that define its function; from tokens, to smart contracts, to block rewards and many other specific functions that govern the operation of the network. The developers of Ethereum built the software to be flexible. Implementation of new rules is possible. The Ethereum foundation has process to propose and implement improvements or changes to the platform using Ethereum Improvement Proposals (EIPs). This process allows for thoughtful and careful updates to the functions of the network. Some of the more famous EIPs involve new functions:

EIP-20 proposed the inclusion of the ERC-20 token standard. This EIP alone has enabled the entire token ecosystem, Initial Coin Offering (ICO) model and decentralized exchanges. The ability to create a cryptocurrency without creating an entire blockchain has massively altered the landscape and lowered the barriers for adoption.

EIP-720 proposed the creation of the ERC-721 Non-Fungible Token (NFT) standard. This standard has enabled an entirely new model of representing objects with value on the blockchain. NFTs are the industry buzzword in 2021, with decentralized exchanges popping up and allowing users to purchase and 'own' NFTs of artwork, music, and other things. Further development of these concepts could lead to real-life integration of physical objects as NFTs, either on the public blockchain or by private companies looking to create - for instance - an internal inventory management system using blockchain technology.

What are Ethereum protocols?

A protocol is a standardized method for performing some action. Ethereum protocols typically designate how the platform will function, and they are named after the proposal that initiated them. Some of the more famous Ethereum protocols are:

ERC-20: This standard defined the mechanism for smart contracts and token distribution, and essentially changed the world of cryptocurrency forever. Instead of developers needing to write their own software, set up their own nodes, and run their own blockchain, now a token developer need only be familiar with the programming language used by Ethereum to define how their token will function within the ERC-20 framework.

ERC-223: This standard improved upon the transfer functions designed in ERC-20, especially with regard to unsupported tokens being transferred to smart contracts. Now, if a token is unsupported, the transaction is canceled. This helps reduce the risk of sending the wrong token to the wrong contract, and potentially suffering the loss of the tokens involved.

ERC-721: This standard introduced the prospect of individual tokens that are not interchangeable with all the other tokens defined by the contract. As such, this standard defines NFTs, which has led to a whole new collection of Dapps that are organized around the sale and holding of NFTs, which themselves hold value and can be collectible.

Ethereum protocols are always being improved upon to increase the security and utility of the network. As such, the Ethereum foundation provides them for review at their website https://www.ethereum.org.

What is Ethereum's ledger?

A ledger, in classical financial nomenclature, references a document that stores financial transactions. A business' ledger is an absolutely critical component of financial record keeping, ensuring historical honesty and integrity for the business against audits.

Ethereum, and all blockchain enabled technologies, automatically store the ledger in the blockchain. The ledger is available for all to see, either through direct analysis of the chain on a node, or through the use of a blockchain explorer. The most common explorer available for Ethereum is https://etherscan.io, though there are others that are available.

Navigating the blockchain explorer allows you to search for blocks, transactions, or addresses with a unified search tool. Everything is cross-referenced, so you can look up a block, see the transactions, click a transaction hash, and then see the addresses that participated in the transaction.

What kind of network is Ethereum?

Ethereum exists as a peer-to-peer (P2P) network, which is the primary architecture for most decentralized cryptocurrencies. Many other platforms use a client/server model, where one or more centralized servers act as a source for data or services. In the P2P model, all synchronized nodes are equal in their operation, and there is no central authority of any kind. Each node establishes connections to several other nodes, providing a robust redundancy and reliability inherent to the P2P model.

How does Ethereum deal with inflation?

Because Ethereum has no maximum supply defined in its supply, it is inherently vulnerable to inflationary effects over time. With each new block, new Ether is emitted into the network which - all other things being equal - reduces the value of each Ether. Recently, updates to the platform to help prepare for Eth 2.0 have implemented burning of Ether with each block. The London Hard Fork implemented the EIP-1559 upgrade, which introduced the burning of the base transaction fees - the minimum amount required to pay for a transaction on the network. With each block, the base transaction fees for each transaction in that block will be burned. The amount burned will vary based on network usage, but at the time of this writing approximately twelve thousand ETH per twenty-four hour period is being burned, equaling almost fifty-five million dollars. These new mechanisms provide a powerful deflationary influence to the platform. When scalability increase comes in Eth 2.0 to permit more transactions occur per second, it is anticipated this burn mechanism may easily increase the amount being burned - assuming no future changes to the burn rate. Because the Ethereum Foundation manages the functionality of the platform through an open proposal system, it is possible to manage the burn rate and emission rate over time to ensure a good value proposition for holders and network participants.

What is the block height of Ethereum?

All blockchain based systems generate a block of data that builds on the previous block. The transactions in block 30 are confirmed and validated by the subsequent blocks. A cryptocurrency client will generally not allow funds to be spent that have not been confirmed by several blocks; which can take some time, depending on the platform. The block height refers to how many blocks have been generated since the so-called 'Genesis' block, which is the first block generated on the network. At the time of this writing, the Ethereum network has generated 13,489,434 blocks - and this is referred to as the 'block height' of the network. Every fifteen seconds, or so, for Ethereum the block height will increment by one. As the block height increases, the blockchain database that is stored by the platform nodes increases in size. Creating a new node, then, over time becomes a progressively longer process as the node must download the entire blockchain before it can be an active participant in the network.

Does Ethereum use atomic swaps?

Atomic swaps are trades that directly swap coins or tokens from separate chains. In the case of Ethereum, where multiple native tokens are supported on the chain, atomic swaps can also be used to trade between tokens on the Ethereum chain. Atomic swaps are specifically a feature of Decentralized Finance (DeFi) systems, which offer peer-to-peer automated trading functionality. Traditional centralized exchanges that follow crypto pair model (BTC/ETH, BTC/DOGE, etc) do not implement the concept of atomic swaps. Atomic swaps are not necessarily a feature of any individual cryptocurrency, but are definitely a feature provided by a variety of exchange services in the decentralized finance space.

A lot of automation and smart-contract style functionality is required to successfully implement atomic swaps. In order to safeguard users, the swapping mechanism has to ensure a series of conditions are fully met before allowing the swap to proceed. Additionally, the swapping mechanism will ensure that the swap reverses if not completed in a timely fashion.

If all of the required conditions are met, however, the swap interface will present you with the price information and the anticipated amount of the other cryptocurrency you will receive, along with a minimum amount that you may receive in the event of price changes. If the price changes rapidly enough such that the minimum amount cannot be delivered in the swap, the exchange will cancel the transaction.

What are Ethereum mining pools?

The difficulty of mining for any cryptocurrency increases over time, if the coin is successful. As more and more miners provide mining capacity to the network, the network will automatically increase the difficulty in order to ensure that blocks are not found too quickly. As this occurs, groups of miners will pool their hardware resources together into mining 'pools'. The pools are typically managed by a centralized software that is quite separate from the network nodes or clients. Each piece of mining equipment that is part of a pool will receive work to process with the goal of solving the current block. If a block is solved by a different miner or group, then new work is distributed to the hardware in the pool. If the block is solved by the pool, then the reward is divided up proportionally to the pool based on amount of contribution made. For instance, a pool made of up ten miners owned by one person, and five miners owned by another will usually give more reward to the person who owns the larger amount of hardware. Some pools may provide a bonus to the miner that actually solves the block. Traditionally, miners are also rewarded for participation over time; if a new, large amount of mining power joins the pool and suddenly starts solving blocks, the other miners will still receive a larger reward for their longer-standing membership in the pool. This helps to provide a fair and balanced reward system for all who participate in the pool.

Who are the largest Ethereum miners?

Typically the largest miners are actually mining pools that generate blocks based on the joint work of many individual miners with their own equipment. The Ethereum block explorer allows for addresses to have a name tag, and so it becomes helpful to look at the blocks as they are generated to see who is mining them. The most recent blocks at the time of this writing indicate the following groups are providing a large amount of mining power to the network (some groups mined multiple blocks, but are listed here only once):

1) F2Pool Old
2) Flexpool.io
3) BTC.com Pool
4) MiningPoolHub
5) Hiveon Pool
6) Ethermine
7) Binance Pool
8) Antpool 2

Other mining pools or individuals may find blocks that are not tagged with a name, and their record looks like this in the block explorer:

1) Miner: 0xcd4...f9c

2) Miner: 0x8f0...be7

Thanks to the anonymity afforded to users of cryptocurrency, unless these addresses are published elsewhere as being associated with an individual or group, it is difficult to say who they are.

As difficulty and competition increase, it becomes harder for an individual to stay profitable based on the cost of equipment and electricity. It makes more sense, then, to pool their resources to gain smaller payouts more frequently than to hope for a single big payout that may happen far less frequently. Hence the majority of mining of any mature or popular cryptocurrency is done via pools.

Is Ethereum technology outdated?

Ethereum is going to be 7 years old in July of 2022, and the core principles that it operates on will be even older. In the lightning speed of the technology world, this is quite old and would normally be considered outdated or obsolete.

Since Ethereum exists primarily as a software platform, and because the original design was intended to be extensible, many updates have been proposed and implemented to keep Ethereum current and relevant in the current cryptocurrency environment. With the move to ETH 2.0, which will further increase the scalability of Ethereum while reducing environment impact, it should stay relevant for the foreseeable future. Therefore, though it is a mature platform, it is not outdated - but has been well designed in order to stay current.

Are there multiple types of nodes?

The Ethereum network recognizes three types

of nodes that individuals can use to support the network.

1) **Full node:** A full node stores the complete blockchain, and participates in block validation and verification, and provides full service to the network and clients on the network. Requires enough local storage resources to accommodate the blockchain. Size requirements increase with the age of the network, and can reach hundreds of gigabytes.

2) **Light node:** A light node stores only the blockchain headers, which is sufficient to provide validation of data, but not to participate in the network in the same way a full node can. This type of node is most useful on resource-constrained devices such a smartphones or low power systems.

3) **Archive node:** An archive node stores the full blockchain, as with the full node, and can perform the same network services. However, the archive node also maintains data on the state of the blockchain at each block level. This additional data allows for lookups of transactions and balances without needing to rescan the entire chain from the genesis block. This is useful for block explorers or

other tools that access snapshots of the chain at points in time. Providing this additional data requires more substantial resources, with storage needs potentially of multiple terabytes.

How does the supply mechanism of Ethereum work?

The Ethereum network emits additional Ether into the network with each new block produced. The creation of new Ether is called 'minting'. A block is produced roughly every fifteen seconds, so new Ether is being minted all the time. Many cryptocurrencies have what is called an 'emission curve' which defines the emission rate over time. Most commonly, the amount of new currency is automatically reduced at various milestones. Bitcoin is famous for its 'halving', which reduces the block reward in half.

Ethereum has no automatic emission model, nor does it have a maximum emission after which no Ether can be emitted. It is infinitely inflationary, in that the network will continue to emit Ether as long as people keep participating in the network (via mining or staking). However, amount that can be produced per year has a cap. If this cap is reached every year, the amount of inflation increase will become smaller year over year because the cap is a smaller percentage of the total supply, even if no burning occurred.

The actual emission per block is governed by the updates to the network and is controlled by the Ethereum foundation. For instance, the initial block emission was 5 ETH, which was subsequently reduced to 3 ETH, and at the time of this writing is around 2 ETH. Block rewards are paid to the miners or pools, where the reward would be divided between the participating miners according to their level of participation.

How is the market cap of Ethereum calculated?

The market capitalization, or 'market cap' is a popular metric for measuring the overall value of a cryptocurrency. It is calculated by taking the circulating supply of a currency, and multiplying it by the current price per unit. This calculated dollar value can serve to help rank and compare cryptocurrencies. The 'fully diluted' market cap is a variation on the calculation. It takes the total supply and multiplies it by the current price. This is helpful to know as this can help gauge where a currency will land amongst the rankings when the emission of coins or tokens is completed. Coin burnings or other functions that affect market cap may not always be known to the ranking websites, and therefore it may require additional research in order to fully compute a market capitalization for a given cryptocurrency.

Can you give and get Ethereum loans?

Yes, there are Decentralized Finance (DeFi) groups out there that will allow you to contribute Ethereum for loaning purposes and receive interest on the amount of you contribute. You can also receive a loan of stablecoins based on a specific amount of Ethereum collatoral that you put up. As with any loan mechanism, it is reasonable to look over the terms of the loan and ensure that the agreement is one you can live with. Ensure the loan site you choose is reputable and secure. Some popular ones such as youhodler.com and aave.com will provide loans and deposits for many mature and popular cryptocurrencies.

What are the largest problems with Ethereum?

Ethereum is a substantial first generation smart-contract cryptocurrency platform. As such, it pioneered many new concepts that have been refined by subsequent platforms. Nevertheless, some issues with scalability are an issue with Ethereum - specifically the transaction lag that occurs due to congestion. The congestion means that a transaction may be delayed due to other, higher priority transactions that have been submitted. This can have an impact on using Ethereum for purchases or trading. Additionally, the congestion results in an increase in transaction fees. It can become very expensive to send a relatively small amount of Ether to another address.

Both of these issues, lag time and transaction fees, are highly visible to the users of the network, and affect user satisfaction with the platform. That said, the Ethereum foundation has plans to implement the sharding mechanism which will allow for horizontal scaling of the Ethereum network into multiple chains that work together and allow for a much higher volume of transactions, which substantially improve user experience as well as reduce transaction fees.

Does Ethereum have coins or tokens?

Yes! The Ethereum platform uses Ether or ETH as it's primary coin. ETH is the coin that powers transactions on the Ethereum network, and it carries fiat value in the same way that Bitcoin does. However, Ethereum also supports a wide and powerful token ecosystem based off of the smart contracts. Essentially, anyone who has some ETH and the know-how to program a contract can generate their own token on the Ethereum network. At the time of this writing, the top tokens by market capitalization on the Ethereum network are:

* Dai (DAI)
* Enjin Coin (ENJ)
* The Sandbox (SAND)
* Centrifuge (CFG)

The power of Ethereum is in that it can provide the foundation for any number of tokens, each with their own unique 'tokenomics' - the fundamentals of how the token works, including supply, distribution, and smart functions. These individual tokens have their own values and market capitalizations that are independent of the ETH value and market capitalizations.

Can you earn money just by holding Ethereum?

Many coins and tokens provide a yield based on how much you hold in your wallet. Others require you to take some action, such as 'staking' in order to reap rewards from the amount you have. Ethereum, currently, does not provide any reward for just holding it. In the near future, Ethereum 2.0 will allow for staking. Staking Ethereum under the new model will result in participants receiving rewards as the network processes transactions and generates new blocks. For those that do not have enough Ether to stake in a solo fashion, staking pools are available that will allow users to stake what Ether they do have and receive rewards in proportion to their contribution.

Does Ethereum have slippage?

Slippage is a market concept that represents a change in value from when an order was placed. In the DeFi world, slippage is an expected thing when dealing with automatic trading sites such as Uniswap. When swapping tokens on the Ethereum network, the trading interface will show the expected amount of token you should expect to receive for your Ethereum. In the time it takes for the transaction to occur, the expected amount may change - for better or for worse. As such, these sites include a setting that allow you to set the amount of slippage that is acceptable. Based on this setting, the trading interface will also show the minimum amount of token you will receive in a worst-case scenario. If the price change results in unacceptable amount of slippage, then the transaction will be canceled.

In the Ethereum world, then, slippage is definitely something to be aware of and consider when making trades of any kind. In a traditional trading interface, it is possible to set a 'Limit' order which helps the trader minimize the possibility of slippage very precisely.

What Ethereum acronyms should I know?

Cryptocurrencies often have a vocabulary all their own. Some of these acronyms are universal, while others (such as GWEI) are very specific to Ethereum.

ATH: All Time High - This is the highest price of a given cryptocurrency during a specific timeframe, or from the beginning of the currency being tracked.

ATL: All Time Low - This is the lowest price of a given cryptocurrency during a specific timeframe, or from the beginning of the currency being tracked.

DAO: Decentralized Autonomous Organization - this is a company or other organization that uses the blockchain to provide governance from all the investors in the DAO. DAO investors hold tokens associated with the DAO and can vote on projects, fund initiatives, or elect individuals to run the DAO. The votes are cast and are proportional to the investors holdings.

Dapp: Decentralized Application - this can be as simple as a smart contract with a web interface, but can turn into complex DeFi interfaces that permit interaction with multiple blockchains and tokens.

DeFi: Decentralized Finance - This is a new type of application enabled by blockchains with smart contracts. It enables a variety of end-user features and applications without using a centralized exchange.

EIP: Ethereum Improvement Proposal - these are proposals administered through the Ethereum Foundation that, upon approval, are implemented in the Ethereum software and chain. They may be as simple as adjusting the rules of reward and burning, or as substantial as defining a new class of token, such as NFTs.

EVM: Ethereum Virtual Machine - this is the

mechanism whereby smart contracts and other automations are able to run on the Ethereum network. The nodes on the network process instructions and incorporate the results into each new block.

GWEI: GigaWEI - This represents a denomination of Ether, and is usually used to help represent gas prices. 10^9 WEI represents 1 GWEI, and 10^9 GWEI equals 1 Ether.

ICO: Initial Coin Offering - an opening sale of a new cryptocurrency. Often these are not based on mining, but are staked. If they are based on mining, then the coins offered under ICO are 'pre-mined', that is mined before the general public is able to mine.

NFT: Non-Fungible Token - These are a token that is completely unique and non-interchangeable with other tokens. Each one represents a single element on the blockchain. They can be used to represent digital artifacts or real objects and can track ownership of them.

PoS: Proof-of-Stake - A consensus method for cryptocurrency where network participants deposit a portion of their holdings, subject to the network minimum, to let their node be a part of processing transactions. When a node is selected for the generation of blocks and processing of transactions, then the reward is paid to that staker.

PoW: Proof-of-Work - A consensus method for cryptocurrency where network participants use high-powered hardware (CPU, GPU, or ASIC) to compete to find the correct block 'nonce'. The winner generates the new block and processes the transaction, and the owner receives the reward. This type of consensus is now considered to be inefficient and environmentally unfriendly; unless certain safeguards have been implements to keep hardware requirements low.

What Ethereum slang should I know?

Ethereum, and cryptocurrencies in general, have their own terminology that is helpful to know in order to understand what people are saying in the forums, chat rooms, and websites that are focused on the crypto community.

51% Attack: This term refers to an attack where a group contains more than half of the nodes running the network. This can allow nefarious people to reverse transactions and double spend tokens or coins. This type of attack is more common on a network that has not reached substantial adoption.

Bag: The amount of any cryptocurrency(ies) held. Your position is your bag.

Bag Holder: Holding a position in a now-worthless coin, e.g. left holding the bag.

Diamond Hands: This term became popularized by the populist investor movement that implies a hard-core unwillingness to sell a position.

DYOR: Do Your Own Research - a quick way to let someone know that they should check into something fully, and not act on whatever messaging is being presented. E.g. "I really like Ethereum and think you should invest, but DYOR."

FOMO: Fear Of Missing Out. This acronym reflects the anxiety people tend to get when they see a stock or cryptocurrency going up and their position is not as big as they would have hoped.

FUD: Fear, Uncertainty, Doubt. This acronym refers to bad or skeptical news that may pop up on message boards or chat rooms. Sometimes the news is legitimate, sometimes not, but often any negative viewpoint is characterized as FUD by those who keep a positive outlook on their positions.

Flippening: The much anticipated, but very unlikely event in which the Ethereum market cap will exceed Bitcoin's.

HODL: A mis-spelled HOLD, often acronymized as 'Hold On for Dear Life'. It's pronounced 'Hoddle'. This statement is a battle cry not to sell in the face of bad news, during a panic selloff, or outright crash. Sometimes leads to bag holders.

Moon: This implies strong upward price movement of a specific cryptocurrency, as though the currency were a rocket going 'to the moon'.

Pump and Dump: A coordinate information and buy/sell method to dramatically increase the price of a given cryptocurrency. Those running the scheme will sell out at the top, and leave many people holding their bag or selling at a loss.

Rekt: A newer term describing those who have been the victims of cryptocurrency schemes or pump and dumps. Pronounced 'wrecked', and means the same as the correctly spelled word.

Whale: Animals are often used to represent

holding levels in cryptocurrency. Whales are typically the largest, and have the ability - if they chose - to affect the market with their activities. For instance, a whale choosing to sell their holdings would probably decimate the market - at least temporarily. Too many whales is considered unhealthy and bad for mature growth for most cryptocurrencies.

Can you use leverage or margin to trade Ethereum?

Yes, this is definitely possible on larger exchanges. Many Exchanges will allow you to trade based on leverage, which involves borrowing funds from a third party in order to trade. For instance, trading with 10x leverage when you have a $1,000 US dollar deposit will permit you to trade effectively with $10,000 US dollars, $9,000 of which were borrowed from the exchange or third party. Leverage amplifies potential gains, but also carries substantial risk. Margin trades are the same concept, but described differently. Margin trades typically outline the percentage of deposit required in order to trade.

Only experienced traders, with the ability to cover potential losses should engage in leverage or margin trading. In the regulated finance world, there are rules and safeguards in place to try to prevent inexperienced investors from having massive exposure to loss. In the less regulated cryptocurrency world, Exchanges may have fewer requirements to meet before providing access to leverage or margin trading.

Most large Exchanges such as Binance, Poloniex, and Kraken permit leverage or margin trading. The larger exchanges require residency checks and track location via IP address. As such, it may not be possible to access these or other features in some locations.

Who owns Ethereum?

The principle of 'owning' Ethereum is true only in the sense that we can count the addresses that hold Ethereum. Most of the addresses out have no ownership publicly associated with them, and indeed it is likely that many of the addresses have been lost by their owners and are now completely inaccessible. Certainly this has been the case for Bitcoin.

There are currently 181 million Ethereum addresses documented on the Ethereum block explorer https://etherscan.io. While it is possible for there to be many more valid Ethereum addresses, the ones listed have at one time or another held Ethereum or participated in a transaction. These addresses include addresses tied to exchanges, smart contracts, and individual investors.

How do you read an Ethereum chart?

The most straightforward way to monitor and predict future performance of Ethereum, or any cryptocurrency, is to see the market performance graphically. This is done through the use of charts, which present metrics like market price, volume, and order book in different graphic styles. Many traders have chart styles they prefer to use, and often generate geometrically based prediction based off of price movements.

The most commonly seen chart used to monitor price performance is a line chart. The line chart shows only the price over time; it's easy to read but lacks depth of information. These charts are most commonly seen on sites like coinmarketcap.com, or on 'beginner-level' exchanges like Robinhood. Exchanges such as Binance or TradeOgre, by default, provide more advanced charting capabilities such as the candlestick chart.

A candlestick chart provides more detail about trading over a specific period. Within each subsection, a wide 'real body' that is color shaded shows whether the closing price was higher or lower than the opening price. Most commonly, red and green are used for the shading. Green indicates the price increased, while red indicates the price decreased. Above and below the main marker are smaller lines called 'wicks' or 'shadows'. These markers indicate the high and low points for the trading period. For instance, a red 'real body' with a high upper wick and no lower wick indicates that the price increased after opening (to reach the high point of the wick), and then decreased to some amount below the opening price. The trading period ended without any increase in price, and so no lower wick appears. The candlestick chart is a powerful tool for leveraging performance data, and crucial to understand to be successful in trading.

Other chart styles exist; these primarily either smooth the movement between the trading periods (Heiken-Ashi) or eliminate time domain information altogether (Renga). Both of these types of charts allow for easier spotting of trends by minimizing small random market moves that may not be relevant to overall performance.

Charting Resources

There are several sites available for charting the performance of Ethereum:

TradingView

tradingview.com (best overall, best social)

CoinGecko

Coingecko.com (large number of currencies tracked)

CoinMarketCap

coinmarketcap.com (simple, easy)

CryptoWatch

cryptowat.ch (very established, best for bots)

CryptoView

cryptoview.com (very customizable)

What is an Ethereum bubble?

A 'bubble' in economic terms is when the market value of something increases at a rate that is unrealistic and not associated with a real increase in value. Typically when this happens, some peak is realized in the market and then is followed by a precipitous crash. These can be dangerous to investors who buy in on the way up, as the crash may not be something that is anticipated and can leave a lot of people selling at a loss. Those who choose to hold may have to wait for a long time for the value to recover, if it ever does.

What does "bullish" and "bearish" mean for Ethereum?

These terms are derived from the traditional financial markets, and represent gains or losses. Specifically, when the overall stock market is on a rise, it is referred to as a 'bull' market. If the market is depressed, then it is referred to as a 'bear' market. Typically the swing is roughly 20% from the previous value. A variety of measurements can help define these statements in the context of the market. One can be 'bullish' or 'bearish' on a single stock, market sector, or the entire market based on one's opinion of whether the value will increase or decrease. This should be informed by market research.

For Ethereum, with a price at the time of this writing of around $4,300, it is hard to be bearish on the currency. Upcoming changes to the platform imply the price will only rise. A bearish outlook would imply that the price would fall by 20% or more, and stay low for an extended period. These types of opinions can help inform market actions -

87

one would not necessarily want to invest in Ethereum if they thought it would fall, but may certainly want to invest if the informed opinion is that it will continue to rise in value over time.

Is Ethereum cyclical?

Yes, Ethereum follows the cyclical pattern often seen in other mature cryptocurrencies. Typically, money entering the cryptocurrency market started in the Bitcoin area, and trickles out to other altcoins, including Ethereum.

Ethereum, cyclically, seems to follow a trend of a breakthrough high, followed by a fall back from that high, and then an accumulation (gradual increase) back toward the high. These cycles occur roughly every four years. It is conceivable to invest based on this principal, though outside influences may affect the timing of these cycles, such as delaying the entire sequence, or varying the timing between the stages of the cycle. Because Bitcoin tends to be at the forefront of market activity, analysts may be able to anticipate moves in Ethereum based on Bitcoin, especially if Ethereum activities (such as burning) provide additional pressure in support of the direction Bitcoin is going.

What is Ethereum's utility?

Ethereum, at its basic level, is a cryptocurrency with its own value that can be traded and held for investment purposes. Beyond this, however, the Ethereum platform allows for the development and implementation of smart contracts and distributed applications that power decentralized finance. Ether, the platform's currency, is used as the driving force behind these many features and pays for the transaction fees for the operations that are performed. The features of the Ethereum network enable things like NFT portals, online gaming, third party finance organizations, DAOs, and more. As such, the utility of Ethereum probably outweighs the monetary value of the currency with all the things it enables.

Is it better to hold Ethereum or trade it?

Investing as a rule requires a lot of skill to be an active trader and maintain a profit. It can be easy to be misled by market moves and make the wrong choice; often you can find yourself out of a position just when the price for that coin is starting to rise. Or, on the other hand, you can easily find yourself in a position just when the coin starts to fall. At that point you're just along for the ride because panic selling avails very little.

The most consistent and pain-free option, then, is to hold Ethereum long term. Assuming that it will continue to rise at rate that is satisfactory, then it is safer by far to buy and hold, and possibly only check the market weekly in order to minimize the temptation to start trading it.

Is investing in Ethereum risky?

All investments in cryptocurrency carry an element of risk. Because Ethereum is an established ecosystem and platform with a large use case, it may present less risk as an investment when compared to other cryptocurrencies that may be available. Nevertheless, there is a possibility of substantial loss if there is a volatile period. So the risk is high, but not as high as investing in some alt-coins which - although they may be cheaper, and present even larger potential upsides, are not as established and may fade out altogether.

What is the Ethereum white paper?

Vitalik Buterin's seminal paper, originally published in 2013, is the originating document describing what would later become the Ethereum platform. Entitled 'A Next-Generation Smart Contract and Decentralized Application Platform', the paper provides an in-depth coverage of the state-of-the-art (in 2013) and what new principles Ethereum would bring to the cryptocurrency community. Notably, it introduces the concepts of smart contracts and explains how this improves over the UTXO principles introduced in the Bitcoin platform. Buterin's white paper serves as the roadmap for the entire Ethereum project, and defined the core principles around which the network was built.

What are Ethereum keys?

Ethereum, and most cryptocurrencies, use a set of keys as part of a wallet. A private key, which is a string of randomized letters and numbers, and a public key which is also a string of letters and numbers.

The private key is generated when a user generates a wallet, either through a local client or on the web. The wallet software then takes the private key string and runs it through a series of cryptographic processes to create the public key. The public key may then be further compressed or adjusted to present a wallet address that is used on the network to send or receive funds. The public keys and wallet addresses can be advertised and made public (hence the name), while the private key should never be shared - but it should be backed up in a very secure fashion.

The private key is the only means by which a wallet can be accessed. In some cases, mnemonic phrases are used to generate the private key as well - and in that case the phrase can also be used to access or restore the wallet. The mnemonic phrase and private keys must absolutely never be shared publicly; once someone else has imported those keys into their wallet software, they have full and complete access to any funds and can transfer them out. Once funds are transferred out of a wallet, they cannot be recovered.

The process of generating the public key is considered cryptographically secure. The very long string of characters that make up the private key is processed through hashing functions that present a completely different string of characters. Unless a vulnerability is found in the cryptographic functions at some point in the future, there is no known way to take a public key and convert it back to a private key. The only option is to use brute force techniques to try to recover a private key. The possible number of private keys for Bitcoin or Ethereum is higher than the number of atoms in the universe; with current computer capabilities the time it would take to brute force a private key is longer than the universe has been in existence. As such, the private/public key pairs used in Ethereum are very secure.

Is Ethereum Scarce?

Ethereum's supply model is infinitely inflationary because it is set to continue emitting Ether for as long as the network continues to function. From that perspective, no, Ethereum is not scarce, and with a circulating supply of over 118 million Ether, there is plenty to go around.

However, with the new burning mechanisms that have been implemented, Ethereum is being burned at a rate that greatly improves the inflation situation. As such, the scarcity of Ethereum is increasing and will continue to increase over time as transactions increase and fees are burned. The Ethereum Foundation may make future adjustments to the emission and burn rates to manage the scarcity of the currency.

What are Ethereum whales?

In cryptocurrency, a 'whale' is an entity that holds enough of the specific currency to be able to affect the prices of the currency on the market. The amount of currency needed to be classified as a whale will vary based on the currency; as different cryptocurrencies have a variety of supply characteristics. Generally, holding a large percentage of the total supply is sufficient to classify one as a 'whale'.

Using the Block Explorer for Ethereum, it is possible to easily identify addresses that hold a relatively high percentage of ETH. Convenient labels are added to known accounts. For instance, the largest holder of ETH (at 6.77%) is actually a utility address for the operation of the Ethereum network. Some other high-percentage wallets are identified and owned by exchanges. The highest unlabeled wallet hold roughly 1.62%. Because this wallet is unidentified, movement of Ethereum to or from this wallet would be of interest to traders.

Whale wallets are closely watched for activity as they actually hold a great deal of power over the market for a given coin or token. Because the ledger is a publicly exposed record of transactions, the actions of a whale are open for all to see. If the whale is an unknown entity, then speculation on any activity can lead to market distortions that may affect the price.

What does it mean to "burn" Ethereum?

Burning Ethereum, or any cryptocurrency, involves sending the coin or token to an address that is inaccessible by any individual. Since a cryptocurrency wallet is really just a string of letters and numbers, any random string of letters and numbers that meets the formatting rules for an address can receive cryptocurrency. As such, it is very easy to define a wallet that can receive funds with a high level of confidence that nobody else will ever be able to retrieve those funds.

Once the funds are sent to the 'burn' address they are rendered inaccessible. This has the result of deflating Ethereum, because the available supply is now reduced. For instance, the Ethereum address *0x000000000000000000000000000000000000 dEaD* has received over 12,500 ETH at the time of this writing, equal to roughly forty eight million US dollars. Because this unusual wallet address was selected, it would be very difficult indeed to retrieve the private key needed to access those funds, and thus it is generally accepted that any ETH (or other tokens on the Ethereum platform) are 'burned'.

What does it mean that Ethereum is inflationary?

An inflationary currency is one in which, over time, the value of each unit of currency reduces. This can occur due to a number of market forces. In cryptocurrency, inflation is most commonly tied to the amount of currency available. Currencies with a fixed maximum supply, or currencies with a burn mechanism are less likely to be inflationary that currencies without these functions. Ethereum was developed as a cryptocurrency with no maximum supply; that is, as long as the Ethereum network continues and people are mining or staking, the network will continue to produce ETH. This ever-increasing amount of ETH makes Ethereum inherently inflationary, unless compensating actions - such as burns - are taken. The recent London hard fork that took effect in August of 2021 has begun this burn process by automatically burning a percentage of transaction fees in every block. As such, this will aid controlling the inflationary trend of Ethereum. In addition to this, recent updates are gradually reducing the amount of ETH rewarded with each block.

What is Ethereum's volume?

Volume is defined in trading as the number of contracts or shares that change hands during a trading day. Stock X could be said to have a volume of five million, and this metric can help determine if a stock is more volatile, or if there is increasing interest in the stock - either good or bad.

In cryptocurrency, where price per coin can fluctuate rapidly and where trading occurs on a 24/7 basis, the volume is typically portrayed as the fiat value of the cryptocurrency that was traded. For instance, at the time of this writing, the 24 hour volume of Ethereum was listed as twenty million dollars. This indicates that twenty million dollars worth - or roughly four and a half million Ether - changed hands within the last day.

Volume itself is a good way to measure interest in a cryptocurrency. Low volume implies that there is poor interest - nobody to buy or sell. Moderate volume day-over-day implies healthy growth and a stable interest, while high volume - especially sudden high volume - implies volatility, either a price drop or gain that may not be permanent but should be closely watched and possibly acted upon based on other news and information.

How is Ethereum mined?

Ethereum operates currently on the 'Proof-of-Work' mechanism for producing new blocks. Blocks are mined by people who participate in the network with equipment and software designed to rapidly solve mathematical hashes to find a 'nonce', which is the correct answer to a block. Once a 'nonce' is found by a miner, the network accepts that block and rewards the miner according to the rules in force at that time for network rewards.

Ethereum uses a method called 'EthHash' as its mining protocol, which relies heavily on graphics processing units (GPUs) with enough memory available to store the data needed to product the nonce. As such, there is a large cost to entering the Ethereum mining world as the right hardware is mandatory.

Mining pools also exist to allow multiple miners to aggregate their hashing power and receive more frequent, though smaller, payouts that are divided between them.

Can you get USD with Ethereum?

There are various companies and websites available to exchange Ethereum for USD or other fiat currencies. Typically there is a fee for this transaction, and the person seeking to obtain the funds must register and provide identity verification in order to withdraw funds. The identity verification is in place to help minimize criminal activity, and also to provide information to the government for tax purposes. In the United States, one of the most popular sites for trading Ethereum to fiat currency is Coinbase.

What is an Ethereum pair?

When trading, all cryptocurrencies are presented as pairs against other currencies. This is represented as "BTC/ETH" or "USDC/ETH". Typically only stablecoins (coins backed by a fiat currency, such as the US Dollar) and the largest cryptocurrencies are permitted as the first half of the pair. The second half of the pair can be any cryptocurrency supported by the exchange that can be traded against the first half. Primarily Bitcoin (BTC) makes up the first half of most trading pairs. The highest volume of trading for a cryptocurrency is usually found here, even when other first-half currencies are available. Some large exchanges with their own token or currency that is part of their trading ecosystem may also create pairs where the first half of the pair is their own in-house currency.

Other trading pairs may exist when the value difference between the first half and second half is too high. For instance, some coins are so poorly valued that they cannot effectively trade against Bitcoin. Often these are traded against a reliable, yet lower valued, coin such as Litecoin (LTC). So, you may see LTC/ based trading pairs. You would need LTC in your trading account in order to purchase the cryptocurrency represented in the second half. Trading in this fashion often is more complex, because you have to track the performance of LTC, the other cryptocurrency you're holding, and BTC.

Is Ethereum better than Bitcoin?

Ethereum is not necessarily better than Bitcoin. Ethereum is a newer, more complex platform than Bitcoin and is able to provide substantially better utility to users. It is, in this regard, more complex to use than Bitcoin and presents a steeper learning curve to those who would plumb its depths.

Bitcoin is primarily defined by nodes, miners, and traders and is only an ecosystem to itself. Ethereum embodies far more; it enabled smart contracts, tokens, and multiple environments that operate on the Ethereum network. Bitcoin could be envisioned as a passenger train; provided a means to transport people from one station to another. Ethereum would then be a freight train; able to carry any number of cargoes from one station to another, along with all of the logistical support that is necessary for the successful operation of such a network.

Can you buy things with Ethereum?

In general, not a lot of retailers accept cryptocurrency in general, and many of those that do will work primarily with Bitcoin. However, some sites will accept Ethereum.

For instance, the following sites are reported to accept Ethereum as payment for goods on their websites:

1) Overstock.com

2) Digitec Galaxus (largest Swiss online retailer)

3) PizzaForCoins

4) Amagi Metals (precious metal retailer)

Many more, smaller, retailers are accepting Ethereum and other cryptocurrencies for payment.

Is Ethereum a good investment?

If past performance is any indication, Ethereum is a good investment. Over the past year, it has had a higher percentage gain than Bitcoin. While cryptocurrency is a highly volatile investment vehicle, Ethereum has several advantages because it is a network with a large level of utility. So many investments have been made into the function and operation of the network, it seems likely that Ethereum will continue to be good investment, although past price performance is no indication of future gains. The price could stabilize for some time, or even go down due to other factors. Like any cryptocurrency, investing in Ethereum comprises an above average level of risk.

Will Ethereum crash?

Given the rise of Ethereum, both in price and adoption, since its inception it seems unlikely that it would crash. The network sees wide usage by a potentially thousands of underlying tokens, each with their own market capitalization and tokenomics. The prime factors that could lead to crash at this point would be either a major security issue - one so endemic to the core of the platform that it could not be recovered from, or a major global regulatory shift to the cryptocurrency concept. That said, the recent ban on cryptocurrency transactions and mining in China has not affected Bitcoin prices, which have since increased. The only known security issue that would affect the price in a major way, would be if a security flaw were discovered in the system whereby private and public keys are related. Such a discovery, and associated attack, could render the entire extant ecosystem of coins and tokens hostage to any attacker. At this time, no such attack is known to exist and to brute force the key pairs would require more computing power than is feasible. It is anticipated, over time, that changes to the key pair process will need to change in order to maintain security ahead of ever-increasing computer power.

What is Ethereum's PoW system?

Like many cryptocurrencies, Ethereum uses Proof-of-Work (PoW) methods to support the generation of blocks and processing of transactions. All miners engaged in PoW are in a race to find the 'nonce', a numeric representation of the next block. A block with a valid 'nonce' can be added to the chain, while invalid the invalid ones are discarded. In Ethereum, the mining protocol is called EthHash. Unlike Proof-of-Stake (PoS) coins, PoW requires no holding of the currency to participate in the network and receive rewards. Hardware requirements can be substantial; EthHash is particularly memory intensive and requires high-capacity Graphics Processing Units (GPUs) to perform the computations. Other, younger chains with fewer participants typically have lower processing requirements - but typically the reward is worth a lot less too. Mining in general is a highly competitive environment.

What is Ethereum halving?

Unlike Bitcoin, Ethereum has no halving process that has been in place since its introduction. Instead, the emission rate of Ether is governed by the EIP and forking process that defines the rules of the network operation. As such, the emission per block can be reduced. The move to Proof-of-Stake is anticipated to reduce the daily emission by 90%, and with the burning mechanism put in place in the London Hard Fork, the 'effective' halving of Ethereum is substantial and will greatly reduce the inflationary pressure on the network.

Why is Ethereum volatile?

Ethereum volatility tends to track with the cryptocurrency market in general, as it is a more mature and broadly invested platform. Newer and less popular cryptocurrencies are more prone to deep swings on their own that do no track with the cryptocurrency market as a whole. That said, the cryptocurrency market is generally volatile. In many countries, the market is highly unregulated. Cryptocurrency is often associated in the news with theft, extortion, and other negative aspects. More recently, government actions have effectively banned cryptocurrencies in some countries which can have drastic effects on prices.

In addition to these directly identifiable price pressures, the world of traditional finance can have an effect on the price as well. As real-world jobs pay more over time, individuals with more disposable income may begin investing in cryptocurrencies, which may cause an increase in prices. Individuals may be more inclined to poor trading strategies - for instance, panic selling - which may contribute to volatility. At times, during periods of bull markets, individual investors have leveraged real-world assets in order to purchase cryptocurrencies. This often happens to late in the run to be profitable, and they may be forced to sell at a loss. This type of unstructured investment contributes to volatility by driving the price up.

Should I invest in Ethereum?

While investing in Ethereum and cryptocurrencies carries a level of excitement, it also carries substantial risk. So, only you can decide if investing in Ethereum is right for you.

That said, Ethereum is a highly mature cryptocurrency that may have less risk than some of the other cryptocurrency options. From that perspective, Ethereum is a good investment. Ethereum has shown a general trend of increase in value over its existance, but continues to be volatile and subject to downturns that may result in financial losses.

The most suitable thing to do when considering any investment vehicle is to research the topic thoroughly and understand all of the possible outcomes when investing. This book, as well as other resources available on the Internet can provide that education. Nevertheless, certain common-sense rules apply, such as - don't mortgage your house to buy cryptocurrency! There have been reports of this and, sadly, they seem to happen when the market is at its peak. Learn to recognize the peaks and avoid investing at those moments. Fear Of Missing Out (FOMO) is another factor to be aware of, and can drive bad investment timing. It is important to maintain objectivity and invest on only sound principles in projects you believe in. There are always memecoins that go up for no reason, but unless you want to hold those for the fun of it, they may not be the soundest financial investment.

How do I successfully invest in Ethereum?

The most crucial elements to successful investing in Ethereum, or any cryptocurrency, is to keep your head. Do your research in advance, including the information in this book, and also with recent news that may impact Ethereum.

Once you have invested, it is important not to make knee jerk reactions to market moves; if the market drops, don't panic sell. If the market starts to rise precipitously, carefully consider whether you want to capture your profits. Don't start buying in out of FOMO when the market starts to rise.

Additionally, investment in other projects that you've researched and checked thoroughly will help diversify your holdings and reduce risk, which is crucial for successful long-term appreciation of your portfolio. There are many other investing focused books that will provide even more principles that will aid in successful investing in any asset.

Does Ethereum have intrinsic value?

There is no intrinsic value in Ethereum, or any cryptocurrency that is not-cash backed. While there are cryptocurrencies that are theoretically backed by fiat currency (the governance of those coin mandates the coin foundation hold fiat currency equivalent to the amount of cryptocurrency in their platform), most pure cryptocurrency platforms are not. The value is generated strictly by users desire to participate in the platform, and is governed primarily by traditional laws of supply and demand. There is no value in the coin or the network except that which is agreed upon by the users. Many national currencies operate in this same way since they are decoupled from any real-world commidity, such as gold. Without an official backing commodity, a fiat currency is worth only what the participants in that economy agree to.

Does Ethereum get taxed?

There is no built-in taxation function in Ethereum, or any other cryptocurrency, except for the fees charged for performing transaction on the network. Taxation, in the traditional sense, occurs when withdrawing ETH, or other cryptocurrencies, to fiat currency. The government regulates which entities are able to perform these withdrawals, and mandates a rigorous identification process so that users who cash out their Ethereum will pay the appropriate taxes to the appropriate state and national entity. Exchanges that are allowed to process withdrawals will provide tax documents to the users to be presented at tax time.

Does Ethereum trade 24/7?

Yes. All cryptocurrencies that are exchange-listed are tradable on a 24/7 basis. This is due in part to the international nature of the cryptocurrency platforms, and also in part because the virtual platforms are decoupled from any business that operates on a standard workweek. Comparatively, most stock exchanges operate during business hours from Monday to Friday. In this case, most businesses operate on the same schedule and announcements that can affect stock prices would in most cases occur doing those times. Cryptocurrencies, on the other hand, can have performance affecting events at any time, and thus are available to trade at any time. This can lead to complexity in trading Ethereum, as an event could happen overseas that has a negative price effect while a large portion of traders are asleep. Limit orders, stop loss, and other tools are available on exchanges to help mitigate some of these issues.

Does Ethereum use fossil fuels?

Ethereum does not inherently use any type of fuel. However the various systems on the Ethereum network (nodes and miners) will likely use whatever locally available electricity is available. It is very likely that large number of these systems are using fossil-fuel based electricity. Individuals or groups running nodes or miners may opt to use solar or wind energy where such options are available to them. Generally, the Proof-of-Work (PoW) system that currently is used for block generation is very power hungry. This is similar to how Bitcoin is considered a very power-hungry network with regard to block generation. The upcoming transition to Proof-of-Stake (PoS) block generation is expected to significantly reduce the carbon footprint of the entire network, and make Ethereum as a platform more competitive with other systems that have come on the scene, touting themselves as a more 'green' option.

Will Ethereum hit $10k?

Ethereum, along with Bitcoin and other popular cryptocurrencies, has seen a meteoric rise - and some dramatic falls - in its relatively short life. Currently, the all-time-high (ATH) of ETH is around $4,300. The easiest way to asses future price potential is to look at the market capitalization of a given coin.

Market Capitalization = Current Price * Circulating Supply

At the time of this writing, the market capitalization of ETH is around $447 billion dollars. With the current circulating supply, a price of $10k would lead to a market cap of over $1.1 trillion dollars, which is in Bitcoin territory. Because Bitcoin only has a max supply of 21 million BTC and a current circulating supply of around 18 million BTC, it is able to support substantially higher price per BTC. Ethereum, with its much higher circulating supply, may take some time to reach the $10k price point. However, recent changes to the burn model of Ethereum in 2021 have resulted in the burning of a portion of the rewards for each block. This means that, over time, the circulating supply will reduce. This will have a largely deflationary effect with positive upward pressure on the price, all other things being equal. $10k is definitely a possibility with this recent development.

Will Ethereum hit $100k?

As previously discussed, the market capitalization calculation provides a fair assessment of the likelihood of any given cryptocurrency reaching a certain price. Since we know that, given the current circulating supply, a ETH value of $10k would present a market cap of roughly $1.1 trillion, we can say that an ETH value of $100k would present a market cap of roughly $11 trillion. This market capitalization would be in excess of the entire top-10 list of cryptocurrency, and as such isn't very likely.

The circulating supply is the largest factor

126

governing this price point. Currently, there are roughly 118 million ETH in circulation. In order for a $100k price point to produce a realistic market capitalization, it seems likely that 100 million ETH would need to be burned. This would still present a larger market cap than Bitcoin; however as the Ethereum network does provide more utility around its financial ecosystem, it may well be worth it at that price point. It seems unlikely such a burn would occur; and further because Ethereum has no emission limit (the total number of ETH to be produced is infinite), eventually the supply would again work against the price. A future price of $100k seems unlikely.

Will Ethereum keep going up this fast?

It seems unlikely that the monumental price increases experienced across all cryptocurrencies will persist, at least for the more mature platforms such as Bitcoin and Ethereum. To use an analogy from the finance world, it is often easier for a penny stock to 100x than a 'regular' stock to 2x. With the maturity and broad exposure that is now part of Ethereum, while increases in the price are expected and desirable, a meteoric rise is unlikely and may not be healthy for the financial aspects of the platform. Large rises often imply high volatility, and traders may begin selling off to claim their profits which could result in second-order effects that would be hard to predict.

What are Ethereum forks?

A 'fork' in a blockchain is when a change to the chain or node software occurs that renders the new blocks in some way different than the old blocks. The old blocks are still valid, but something new or different exists in the new blocks that differentiates them.

In many cases, forks can cause issues. If not all nodes on a cryptocurrency network are prepared for the fork, the unprepared nodes may carry on with the outmoded chain and continue to generate blocks that are incompatible with the main chain. In a sense, this is a different cryptocurrency - at least for a time. Bitcoin Cash is a fork of Bitcoin, and in fact shares part of the chain up until the split. You can look up early Bitcoin addresses on both networks, and in fact the same address can have both BTC and BCH coins in the wallet, depending on when it was deposited.

Why does Ethereum fluctuate?

As with any stock or other cryptocurrency, the prices of Ethereum are governed by the availability of the asset for purchase and the demand for it. As more people compete to purchase Ethereum, the price goes up. If fewer people are looking to purchase, and more people are looking to sell, the price will fall to make it more competitive.

Aside from traditional supply and demand metrics, the unregulated crypto market operates on a 24/7 schedule. News or events can be released at any time that may affect investor confidence or enthusiasm, causing price fluctuations and volatility at unexpected times. The entire cryptocurrency family also tends to move together in price, such that bad news on unrelated currencies could have a negative impact on Ethereum, even though the same news has no real impact on the Ethereum network or utility. This phenomenon may have less impact over time as each currency becomes more accepted as its own entity as opposed to being lumped together under the umbrella of 'crypto'.

How do Ethereum wallets work?

A wallet is either a program or website that interfaces with the Ethereum network. It allows the end user to see their addresses, perform transactions, and generate new addresses. A wallet program may store its data in a local file that you can encrypt for safekeeping and import to other workstations. The web wallet typically does not allow direct access to the file that actually contains the wallet data. Almost every cryptocurrency has a custom program that you can use as a wallet, and the web-based wallets comes later as the platform gains adoption. Exodus and Coinbase are both highly regarded web wallets that support multiple cryptocurrencies and allow you to view your holdings in aggregate. MyEtherWallet is a convenient web wallet specifically targeting Ethereum users which allows for management of your Ethereum and Ethereum tokens. In every case, it is highly recommended to take copious backups of your wallet and/or mnemonic phrases in order to be able to recover your wallet if it is ever lost. Never share your private key with another individual, as they could easily steal any funds you have in the associated wallet.

Does Ethereum work in all countries?

Yes! Ethereum as a platform and currency should work in every country. There is no technical restriction in the system that would prevent it from working anywhere there is Internet access.

In recent months, some countries have begun a crackdown on the ability of users to trade or mine cryptocurrency of any kind, Ethereum included. In these cases, political factors may prevent people from easily participating in the Ethereum environment. It may require greater ingenuity or technical skills in order to trade or mine Ethereum in those cases; specifically VPNs may be needed in order to minimize the possibility of monitoring by authorities

How many people have Ethereum?

At the time of this writing, there are roughly 182 million Ethereum addresses that have been registered on the blockchain. This means that at one time 182 million addresses have been sent or received Ether, but some of them may be empty by now. That said, a recent statistic from bitinfocharts.com showed that only 865,709 addresses were actually active. This statistic would not include long term holders who do not regularly send or receive Ethereum. Since individuals may have multiple Ethereum addresses, and many addresses out there are held by exchanges or smart contracts, it is probably safe to say that the number of people who actually have Ethereum is much smaller than the number of addresses. An older study from Cambridge indicated that, at that time, 3 million people worldwide actively held Bitcoin or Ethereum. The fact is, however, that with the recent advent of stock brokerages such as Robinhood making crypto available to customers, the actual number is much much higher. Over one million people have expressed interest in joining Robinhood's crypto exchange.

We can say, then, that generally the number of people holding crypto is certainly in the millions, and Ethereum is no exception based on the number of wallet addresses out there and the activity on the platform.

Who has the most Ethereum?

The Ethereum blockchain explorer, etherscan.io, provides an at-a-glance view of the accounts that have the most Ether. The highest two, respectively, are smart contracts for the Eth2 Deposit Contract, which is the deposit location where users who are participating in the Proof-of-Stake (PoS) mechanism need to sent their Eth. This account represents 7.42% of the total ETH held in all accounts.

The second runner up is the contract account for the Wrapped Ether token. This token is used in automations and DeFi applications, and is equivalent in value to Ether. In many cases, smart contracts operate with tokens instead of native cryptocurrency, and so this 1-to-1 token serves that same purpose. For anyone who has Wrapped Ether (WETH), they can swap their WETH for ETH, which should reduce the amount of ETH held in this contract address. The WETH contract address accounts 6.2% of all ETH held.

The third and fourth entries, at roughly 1.6% apiece are Exchange holdings for Kraken and

Binance. These groups have other accounts as well, so these two wallets are not representative of all ETH held by those two exchanges.

Beyond this small list, it is possible that other individuals or groups have substantial Ether holdings divided up into multiple wallets. Some may elect to use paper or hardware wallets to hold a portion of their ETH, while holding an additional portion of ETH in a web wallet that they use to trade. In those cases, we are not able to add up the wallets to see what someone's total amount of Ether is. No doubt there are people out there with a lot of Ethereum, held in such a way to keep their wealth secret.

Can you trade Ethereum with algorithms?

Yes, it is absolutely possible to use automated trading processes to trade Ethereum and other cryptocurrencies. Several types of models exist to do this, and it requires membership in an exchange platform that supports automated trading input - often through an Application Programming Interface (API).

Some individuals have coded algorithms to allow them to trade on arbitrage. This is where one Exchange may have a different price on a coin or token than another. It is possible to trade, transfer, and trade again quickly enough to make money on these price differences. This process can be automated, but requires two exchanges and is dependent on the price difference being sufficient to overcome fees, etc.

Other algorithm trading mechanism operate within a single exchange and monitor prices within that exchange, performing high speed trades based on smaller price differences. Because cryptocurrency prices are always changing in small amounts, a high speed trading algorithm can potentially leverage smaller price changes to bring reasonable returns.

Of course, a badly designed algorithm could quickly lose a great deal of money. It is important, therefore, to ensure and test assumptions before trading with real Ethereum and ensure that there are safety nets in place to prevent a complete loss.

How will Ethereum affect the future?

Since its inception, Ethereum has pushed the boundaries of cryptocurrencies by implementing intelligence and autonomy into the platform. As such, many similar projects have already been spun up - either as their own platform, or as a side-chain to Ethereum, such as Cardano, Solana, Polkadot, and others. Ethereum introduced the idea of tokens, smart contracts, and NFTs, which have inspired these other groups to incorporate those concepts. Because Ethereum was first, some of the downsides of the Ethereum methods (high gas fees, for instance) have given some incentives for others to build their platforms with lower fees, lower latency, and other improvements that give them a competitive advantage.

The concepts that Ethereum has introduced, and will continue to refine as the platform iterates to stay competitive, may quite literally be world changing. The concept of NFTs, for instance, extend beyond digital artwork and may eventually be a means of owning or trading real physical assets on the blockchain. This would greatly reduce the possibilities of fraud or theft by providing a chain of ownership for anything from real estate, rare coins, airplanes, or even books. These same principles could be extended to verification of authenticity for documents and media, which may help in combat the rising specter of deep-fake videos that can be used to spread false information very convincingly.

Because Ethereum developed more than a store-of-value cryptocurrency platform, the sky is truly the limit with this intelligent and programmable platform.

Is Ethereum the future of money?

Ethereum may not be the future of money itself, but it represents a quantum leap in the improvement of decentralized financial systems for end users. Now users can deposit funds and accrue interest and take out loans outside of the traditional finance systems that are highly regulated and government-tied.

How many people are Ethereum billionaires?

Due to the anonymous nature of cryptocurrencies, it is difficult to estimate how many people may be billionaires based off their Ethereum holdings. Individuals may have two or more wallets, which would split up their holdings. Unless you could know that the same person held two accounts, they could disguise their total holdings very easily.

There are roughly 32 Ethereum accounts with sufficient holdings that would equal roughly one billion US dollars. At the current price of Ether, it would require roughly 250,000 ETH to equal 1 billion US dollars. Many of these accounts are owned by exchanges, smart contracts, and the like - so it seems likely that most of the addresses are not connected to individuals.

Are there secret Ethereum billionaires?

Very likely! Within the top 32 addresses that hold 1 billion US dollars or more, some of the accounts are not tagged with any identifying information. These accounts may or may not be held by individuals.

It is also likely that individuals could have 2 or more Ethereum accounts that they control where the total amount of all the accounts totals more than 250,000 ETH, which equals roughly 1 billion dollars. Two accounts with 125,000 ETH each then, or even 10 accounts with 25,000 ETH could easily be held in secret.

Will Ethereum reach mainstream adoption?

Ethereum is already a very popular platform because of it's maturity and stability. In the future, with the advent of lower fees and improvements to the transaction latency, more and more communities and companies may leverage the possibilities that are available through the use of the Ethereum blockchain. Companies could experiment with inventory systems, customer management services, and any number of software capabilities that can be ported to the Ethereum blockchain. As such, with a lower barrier to entry and better performance capabilities, the adoption should only increase.

Will Ethereum get taken over by other cryptocurrencies?

At the time of this writing, Ethereum is the #2 cryptocurrency in the world, with a market capitalization of almost 500 billion United States dollars. As such, any competing currency would need to reach this level in order to be a serious competitor.

Currently, the closest competitor is the Binance Coin (BNB) with a market cap of almost 88 billion dollars. It would require a 4-5x increase of BNB in order to reach parity with Ethereum; but the Binance Coin is a centralized coin associated with the Exchange. There are concerns amongst many investors over the centralized network model. Ethereum also offers the utility model with the Smart Contract capabilities operated through the Ethereum Virtual Machine, and a substantially more open community that allows for greater participation when compared to Binance.

Moving down the list to the next most valuable coin by market cap is the Tether coin (USDT). This coin is managed centrally by Tether and is intended to be a stablecoin, pegged to real US dollars held by Tether. With a market cap of 76 billion dollars, it too is not a close contender. In order to overtake Ethereum, Tether would have to massively increase their fiat holdings, which while possible, seems unlikely.

Other networks and platforms may someday overtake Ethereum, especially if there were some fatal flaw to be found in the Ethereum platform. With the continuous improvement and evolution being driven by the Ethereum Foundation, it seems unlikely that any other platform will overtake Ethereum any time soon.

Can Ethereum change from PoW?

Ethereum has been working toward a departure from Proof-of-Work (PoW) techniques for awhile. The groundwork has been laid, especially with the London Hard Fork in 2021, to move Ethereum to the Proof-of-Stake model. This is expected to take place either in late 2021 or early 2022, and will involve - among other things - eliminating the PoW algorithm from the platform. Instead, a network of clients - called validators - who have an amount of Ether staked will be selected to validate a block. This will eliminate the hashing requirement and competition that is the heart of many blockchain platforms currently. It will also have the effect of reducing the energy consumption of the platform as a whole but a huge margin, giving Ethereum a boost as a highly adopted currency that is now much 'greener'.

Was Ethereum the first ever cryptocurrency?

The honor of being the first ever cryptocurrency goes to Bitcoin, which was brought into operation in January of 2009. Vitalik Buterin, the programmer behind Ethereum, first worked with Bitcoin and wrote articles about it in 2011, before launching Ethereum in 2015. Including Bitcoin, there are 18 cryptocurrencies that precedes Ethereum; these were released between 2009 and 2015.

Can Ethereum be more than an alternative to gold?

In short, yes. Ethereum provides more than a digital 'store of value' capability. Unlike Bitcoin, which acts strictly as an investment suitable for buying and selling based on price and anticipated market moves, Ethereum provides more. The Ethereum Virtual Machine (EVM) capability make Ethereum a 'smart' financial ecosystem that can create all new currencies that ride on its own chain. As such, the value in Ethereum is at least partly due to the utility of the platform. As such, it seems reasonable to believe that Ethereum represents more than a digital store of value, a digital gold, and is in fact a highly multi-faceted investment that goes beyond traditional financial thinking.

What is the latency of Ethereum, and is it important?

The latency is generally realized as the time between the submission of a transaction and the approval of that transaction in the blockchain. Unlike Bitcoin, Ethereum produces a new block roughly every fifteen seconds. Therefore the blockchain itself presents a rather low latency compare to other platforms.

Latency can become an issue, even with Ethereum, as the transactions begin to increase. Because of the multi-layered nature of the Ethereum platform, where dozens of tokens may also change hands within each block - in addition to native Ether transactions, congestion begins to present itself. Only so many transactions can be performed within a block, and those that are not included must wait for the next block. Additionally, transactions that include additional gas will be prioritized. This means that transactions that pay only the minimum gas fees may have significant lag.

The transaction lag for any cryptocurrency can be important when trading, as the price changes from when a transaction is sent and when a transaction is approved and recorded 'on-chain' could be significant enough to reduce profits, especially when working with arbitrage trading on multiple exchanges. Additionally, since the transaction load and congestion causes a need for higher transaction fees, it becomes more expensive to send Ether for any purpose.

Future improvements to the chain are intended to help with scalability and will, it is hoped, mitigate these issues and permit transactions on a larger scale with low latency.

What are some Ethereum conspiracy theories?

Many areas of the cryptocurrency arena are riddled with a variety of conspiracy theories; often these are tied to issues with altcoins that caused their downfall. Ethereum, though an early pioneer in cryptocurrency, doesn't seem to have any popular conspiracy theories that might affect its pricer performance or operation.

Why do other coins often follow Ethereum?

Ethereum, as the #2 cryptocurrency, is one of the main market bellweathers for all other cryptos. Bitcoin is the more obvious one, being the first and most well known amongst investors. Essentially, money moves between Bitcoin and Ethereum and all other altcoins. Because the exchanges tie everything to Bitcoin, and some coins to Ethereum, all of the alt-coins do tend to follow the market moves of the two primary currencies.

What is Ethereum Classic?

Ethereum Classic is a crytocurrency and blockchain that is based on the same core software as Ethereum. Ethereum Classic came to life as a result of a massive theft on the Ethereum blockchain. In 2016, a group called 'The DAO' was formed to act as a decentralized asset management organization. DAOs can be formed on any similar type of blockchain, and function as a democratically organized investment vehicle where stakeholders can provide governance and direct the investment of the DAOs funds. The acronym has become more generic since 'The DAO' was formed.

Despite warnings of substantial vulnerabilities in the code used to run The DAO's websites and software, the group did not react quickly enough to to warnings and roughly 1/3 of all the invested ETH was moved to a separate account. This accounted for roughly 3.6 million Ether, or a little over one billion United States dollars as valued at the time.

With the prospect a thieves controlling a large amount of Ether, the Ethereum Foundation made the decision to roll the blockchain back in a way that would return the stolen Ether and allow investors to get their money back. Miners and nodes that disagreed with this decision, and supported leaving the Blockchain unaltered, would mine the first Ethereum Classic block at block height 1,920,000. The currency ticker for Ethereum Classic is ETC.

Since then, the Ethereum Classic blockchain has made several policy decisions that showcase a different philosophy toward cryptocurrency than that of Ethereum proper. One such decision, for instance, was the elimination of the Proof-of-Work (PoW) timebomb mechanism that increased mining difficulty. In the Ethereum ecosystem, this was part of the migration to the Proof-of-Stake (PoS) model. The Ethereum Classic group declined to move to PoS, and therefore eliminated the changes to the blockchain that would have made PoW mining more difficult. Ethereum Classic seeks, however, to maintain code compatibility with Ethereum so that on-chain applications can be portable between the two chains.

How will Ethereum act during a recession?

Cryptocurrencies in general perform well during a financial recession. Bitcoin itself was born out of a recession in 2008, and the opportunities in cryptocurrency have only increased since then. Historically, precious metals like gold and silver appreciate in value during a recession because people purchase them as hedge against the stock market, which typically performs poorly or unpredictably during a recession. Many mature cryptocurrencies are seen as a digital gold, and there is further incentive to invest due to the decentralized and anonymous nature of crypto. Since Ethereum has the value added capability of operating as a fully-fledged financial system through smart contracts, staking, etc., it seems likely that a lot of money could move into Ethereum during a recession, making it an ideal place hold funds against economic downturns.

Smaller, less mature cryptocurrencies may not survive a recession because money moves out of them into the more mature options. This has the effect of discontinuing poorly performing platforms, acting as a kind of sieve that helps the stronger platforms remain strong even during a recession event.

Can Ethereum survive in the long run?

The question regarding Ethereum's long-term viability is one that has been discussed at length. High gas prices, lack of a 'green' strategy, and frustration with the poor transaction speed has pushed competitors to bring forward the 'next-generation' cryptocurrency platforms. Groups such as Polygon, Cardano, Polkadot, and Solana represent powerful decentralized cryptocurrency networks that are gaining ground, driven by lower cost transactions, transaction speed, and other powerful features enabled by these improved functions.

With that said, Ethereum's developers have worked hard to keep the Ethereum network competitive with the push toward Eth 2.0. Proof-of-Stake will reduce energy consumption massively, while new blockchain techniques such as 'sharding' will enable parallelization and scalability of transactions. Ethereum's massive market share and name cache should ensure that this rebirth will keep the platform relevant for years to come.

What is the end goal of Ethereum and cryptocurrencies?

There are several goals to Ethereum and cryptocurrencies in general.

1. Cryptocurrencies generally exist to provide a decentralized store of value. The currency can be transferred from account to account for a reasonable fee, in a reasonable time, and anonymously, if desired. In this way, cryptocurrency eliminates the traditional finance infrastructure

2. Cryptocurrencies provide a means of value appreciation, either via holding a given currency in the hops it will appreciate, or to trade it on exchanges in the hopes of growing the amount of currency held by selling high and buying low. In this regard, cryptocurrency cuts out the traditional brokerages and brokerage rules that may limit one's trading options (day trading, for instance, which requires a substantial deposit).

3. Ethereum, and similar cryptocurrency

161

platforms, seek to provide a means of automating financial operations through the use of the Ethereum Virtual Machine functions. This allows for new 'tokens' to be generated and operate on their own independent financial principles, such as automatic burning, automatic redistribution of fees, and the like. It opens the door for experimental financial systems at a scale hitherto impossible.

4. To establish fully independent control over one's own financial assets without the use of any third party institutions, in a fully anonymous fashion.

5. To establish governance mechanisms for investor-driven organizations to exist and to provide a mechanism for voting, distributing funds, and distributing rewards in a completely auditable and self-contained way.

Is Ethereum too expensive to use as a cryptocurrency?

The individual price of Ethereum, or any other cryptocurrency, is largely irrelevant with regard to its utility or value as an investment. While Ethereum is essentially the second highest-price cryptocurrency, and second also with regard to market cap, it also encompasses a larger ecosystem of capabilities that enable large scale decentralized finance. This means that tokens can be minted on the platform that may themselves become valuable, and - conceivably - could exceed the value of Ethereum itself. As it is, the market capitalization is a more effective measure of value as it represents the price per coin multiplied by the number of coins in circulation (or the maximum number of coins, if known). This metric is a much better gauge to use when comparing cryptocurrencies. Each ecosystem is designed differently, with different utility, emission curves, circulating supply, and total supply. The market capitalization helps to normalize all of these variables into a single statistic. For instance, the market capitalization of Ethereum is roughly half that of Bitcoin, but the price per coin of Ethereum is much lower than that of Bitcoin. Nevertheless, the strength of Ethereum can be seen in it's market cap which is currently close to 500 billion US dollars.

When was the Ethereum London hard fork?
The London hard fork occurred in the first week of August, 2021.

Does Ethereum halve?

Halving is a process whereby mining rewards are reduced as a crypto blockchain progresses through time. Bitcoin is most notable for its halving. This process reduces the emission of the platform's coin, increasing scarcity and helping to maintain or increase the price.

Ethereum does not halve. That said, the reward rate is actually manually controlled through the Ethereum Foundation. Ethereum Improvement Proposals (EIPs) are the process whereby changes to the core functionality of Ethereum are proposed, discussed, and accepted into the chain. The reward model for Ethereum has been modified several times throughout the history of the platform. Specifically, EIP-649 in 2017 proposed a reduction of the Ethereum base reward to 3 ETH. EIP-1234 proposed the reduction to 2 ETH in 2018. It has remained 2 ETH since 1234 was implemented. These reductions in the mining rewards affect only the core reward, but the transaction fees were unadjusted until the London hard fork, in which a portion of transaction fees were burned.

Are Ethereum addresses case sensitive?

Ethereum addresses are represented by a 64 character string of hexadmical letters and numbers. Hexademical is a numbering scheme that represents sixteen values per character. It uses 0-9 to represent their usual value, and letters A through F to represent values of ten through sixteen. Most commonly, a hexademical string is prefixed by "0x", which serves only to identify the string as being hexadecimal. An Ethereum address may look like the following:

0xFAF10F834565FF09A08B5406DBAd770794D 1DB2C

The example above has each letter capitalized, but this is not necessary. The address above is the same as this address, where each letter is lower-case:

0xfaf10f834565ff09a08b5406dbad770794d1db 2c

There may be some addresses where some

letters are capitalized, and others are not. This scheme represents a checksum that ensures the address is a valid address:

0xFAF10F834565FF09A08b5406DbAd770794d 1DB2C

Sending ETH to any of these representations will have the same result. The Ethereum network does not care about the case sensitivity when sending coins or tokens. The checksum feature is of benefit, for applications that support it, to help prevent a mistake in sending ETH to an incorrectly typed address. The Ethereum address does not lend itself well to typing, and a copy/paste could easily omit a character at the beginning or end, which would result in an invalid address.

Are Ethereum and Ethereum 2.0 the same?

Ethereum has announced the move to Ethereum 2.0, and with this move comes a lot of functional changes to the platform. Both operate on the same platform, but Ethereum 2.0 is a substantial upgrade to the existing ecosystem.

Ethereum 2.0 focuses on improving key areas of the original product: scalability and efficiency. The upgraded system will move to a Proof-of-Stake type of validation, which will be substantially more power efficient than the existing Proof-of-Work (PoW) mechanism that is currently used. Sharding, which is a major architectural upgrade to the platform, allows for multiple blockchains to exist in the same platform and interoperate with each other. As such, this type of parallelization will allow for major scalability improvements in terms of transaction processing. It should permit a much higher transaction per second rate, which is crucial for accommodating an ever increasing user base.

Are Ethereum coins limited?

Ethereum itself has no defined maximum supply; that is to say that new coins will be minted for as long as the network is in operation. Recent changes that reduce the amount of ETH minted per block, along with transaction fee burning, will help reduce the amount of ETH being produced. Under certain circumstances, it is possible that the currency may become deflationary - in that more coins will be burned than produced over a given timeframe. While not providing a hard limit to the number of ETH, these updates may act as a governing mechanism against uncontrolled inflation.

Are Ethereum mining rigs worth it?

Not at this time. Since its inception, Ethereum has been built around the Proof-of-Work block production mechanism, where miners used a variety of hardware (primarily high-memory GPUs, as Ethereum is ASIC-resistant) to compete to generate blocks and gain the rewards. The reward for finding a block is not insubstantial, at this time it is roughly 2 ETH plus the gas costs for the transactions in the block.

However, the London hard fork introduced new mechanisms designed to help nudge the network toward the Proof-of-Stake model, including an artificial increase in mining difficulty which will occur at block level 200,000. This should occur roughly in December 2021 and make PoW mining almost impossible. As such, investment in new mining rigs is probably not advisable unless there is an intent to mine other cryptocurrencies after the difficulty increase takes effect. There are many other currencies still available that can be profitably mined with the hardware currently used to mine Ethereum, and these will continue to be available for the foreseeable future. Other mining software may be necessary, but often the hardware used for mining Ethereum should continue to be compatible with other platforms. It may also be possible to use the hardware to mine on emerging platforms, which could provide a lot of rewards fairly quickly, with the possible downside that if the new network proves to be a failure, the time spent mining may have been wasted. On the other hand, getting in early on a new currency may reap substantial rewards if the adoption of the platform increases.

Are Ethereum transactions traceable?

Ethereum transactions are traceable, but also party anonymous. Because the blockchain is a public ledger of transactions, all the transactions performed can be easily viewed. This includes transactions of new Ether sent to miners' addresses, smart contract functions, and the like. All transactions are listed, including the fees and other associated metadata that the blockchain needs to know about in order to successfully process and maintain a clean record.

Therefore, an Ethereum transaction is traceable and, in fact, you can 'follow' Ether as is moves from account to account - although it can be mixed in with other balances and transactions, the same as cash can be mixed and redistributed in different amounts. While individual dollar bills have a serial number and can be traced, individual Ether have no such identification. Because of this, individual Ether cannot be tracked.

Additionally, the Ethereum accounts where

Ether is sent or received are anonymous. It is true that some people will tag their account with an identifier in the block explorer, or may have published their addresses with the goal of receiving payment. In those cases, a transaction to that address becomes a non-anonymous transaction. Enough information is available to say that Robert Godfrey, who published their Ethereum address, received 3 ETH on Monday, June 16th. Further research could bring to light Robert's address, phone number, etc. Suddenly an anonymous blockchain is a little less anonymous.

Are Ethereum gas fees fixed?

No, the gas fees are not fixed and can be highly variable depending on the load on the network. Because the Ethereum network can only support up to 30 transactions per second, there is substantial competition for a given transaction to be processed in a timely fashion. As such, individuals can choose to pay additional gas in order to prioritize their transaction. During periods of high congestion, minimium gas fees will rise. It is often strategic, if a transaction is not time-sensitive, to make transactions during hours when congestion is lower in order to pay lower gas fees.

Are Ethereum and Cardano competitors?

It seems likely that Cardano is out to compete with Ethereum in several ways.

1) Cardano was founded by Ethereum co-founder Charles Hoskinson in 2015, after a disagreement regarding for-profit/non-profit status for the Ethereum foundation.

2) Cardano uses a currency called Ada (ADA) that runs on a Proof-of-Stake (PoS) blockchain. Cardano was designed from the ground up to be PoS based, which is the more environmentally friendly model. It also support substantially higher transactions per second than either Ethereum or Bitcoin.

3) The 'Alonzo Hard Fork' in September 2021 introduced the long-awaited smart-contract virtual machine capability into the platform, which allows for feature-parity with Ethereum.

4) Cardano is the largest PoS cryptocurrency by market cap, and is 7th overall according to coinmarketcap.com. That said, price per coin and

overall market capitalization are much lower than Ethereum at this point.

5) Ethereum has been slowly moving toward the Proof-of-Stake model for some time, while Cardano has been moving toward the smart contracts for some time. It seems like a general equality between the two platforms will come about in 2022, if Ethereum's plans for PoS are finalized.

Generally speaking, it seems like Cardano was introduced in order to be sort of an Eth 2.0 well before Eth 2.0 was in the works, which would make it seem to be a competitor - however, with so much infrastructure already built on the Ethereum platform, finding utility for the Cardano network may take years to accomplish.

Are Ethereum transactions anonymous?

Ethereum transactions are anonymous in that they expose only the wallet addresses involved. Ethereum as a platform is inherently anonymous, unless an individual chooses to reveal their wallet address in conjunction with other personally identifiable information such as real name, address, business name, etc. Often people will do this when seeking payment or donations for services, when they choose to take such payments in cryptocurrency.

How do Ethereum smart contracts work?

A smart contract is a scripted program that runs on the Ethereum network. Rather than an end-point on the network being responsible for storing and running the program, the entire network supports the function of the contract as it interacts with the blockchain. They exist as a type of Ethereum account, which means that a smart contract has a wallet address, balance of coins or tokens, and can send and receive transactions programmatically without any user engagement. As users submit coins or tokens to the contract address, pre-programmed functions can take effect and perform any number of activities. Once a smart contract has been defined on the network, they cannot be deleted, and interactions with them are not reversible, e.g. you cannot request a refund of ETH sent to a contract address. A simple smart contract example would be if you sent an amount of ETH to the contract address. The contract would register the receipt of the ETH and automatically send you an equally valued amount of WETH (wrapped ETH, a token on the Ethereum blockchain that hold equal value with ETH).

A smart contract can do substantially more than a basic coin/token swap, of course. Deflationary mechanisms, airdrops, redistribution of transaction fees, and much more are able to be instilled into the blockchain and function autonomously; in fact,

How does Ethereum burning work?

In cryptocurrency, a 'burn' occurs when coins are send to an address that is owned by no entity. The burned coins cannot be retrieved and, by consensus, are considered destroyed. Burns can happen manually or automatically triggered by some action. With the London Hard Fork implemented on the Ethereum platform in August 2021, burning is automatically performed.

Ethereum miners, prior to the fork, had received both the base fee and priority fee for the transactions on the network, in addition to the reward defined per block. With the new operating rules, the base fee is burned. Miners still receive the priority fee (an additional 'tip' added by senders to motivate miners to process their transactions) and the block reward. Since the implementation of the burn, at the time of this writing, over one million ETH have been burned.

How does Ethereum make money?

The Ethereum foundation was initially funded through the sale of Ether in exchange for Bitcoin during the Initial Coin Offering (ICO). Because their development wallet is known, we can also see that they have 353,618 ETH in their wallet, with a current value of over a billion dollars. The foundation itself if a non-profit organization, so their primary goal is to meet expenses and fund further development of the Ethereum platform. Because of the highly decentralized nature of cryptocurrency, it is possible that they pay developers in Ether in addition to fiat currency, and the developers can live almost anywhere in the world, with lower cost of living than would be found in places like the United States.

How is Ethereum different from Bitcoin?

While Bitcoin has the privilege of being first, it is generally a fairly basic platform that is intended to be a digital gold that can be held or transferred. Beyond this, the Bitcoin platform has minimal utility.

Ethereum, on the other hand, represents a highly programmable platform that uses the Ethereum coin (Ether) to power not only transactions, but automatic systems such as smart contracts. In this way, there are limitless ways to interact with the blockchain through apps on the web, smartphone, etc. It is possible to run any number of independent financial systems on the Ethereum network, each one with its own value and rules of operation. As such, Ethereum brings financial depth to the cryptocurrency ecosystem.

How did Ethereum start?

Ethereum was born out of a technical white paper authored by Vitalik Buterin. Buterin worked with a group of individuals to develop the software under a Swiss **company** called Ethereum Switzerland GmbH. Later, Buterin and others formed the Ethereum Foundation, establishing the funding through an Initial Coin Offering (ICO) to fund the development of the software. The network went live in July 2015.

Where does gas go?

Gas fees paid by Ethereum users are paid out to the miners as they successfully create blocks in the blockchain. Until the London hard fork, the gas was paid out in its entirety to the miners. Since the fork, transaction fees are partially burned. This was implemented to begin offsetting the unlimited emission of Ether. As originally conceived, Ether was a highly inflationary currency; over time, with an unlimited emission ceiling, the value of each coin would drop. By implementing an automated burn of some of each transaction fee, this helps the value to stabilize for the future.

Where to stake Ethereum?

As part of the new Ethereum 2.0 push, users with a suitable amount of Ethereum can stake their coins individually. The current requirement to take is 32 ETH. For those who do not have that much, it is possible to use pooled staking services. These pools provide the ability for multiple users to pool smaller amounts of ETH together in order to act jointly as a validator and reap the rewards, subject in some cases to a small fee for the management of the pool. The Ethereum foundation provides a list of current staking services on their website, along with the various requirements each one has defined in order to take. The listing is here: https://beaconcha.in/stakingServices.

Which Ethereum pool is best?

There are a few factors to consider when choosing a mining pool. Specifically, consider pool hash rate, fees, and payout model when considering a pool.

1) Pool hash rate: A pool's hash rate is the aggregate of the hash rate of the participant's mining hardware. A larger pool hash rate will ensure that the pool receives rewards more frequently, as the pool is more competitive on the network. For the individual miner, this can ensure more frequent payouts. However, an individual miner in a larger pool will likely receive a smaller reward as the reward must be split up between more pool participants. Miners who wish to support a healthy, decentralized network may also want to choose a pool that has less overall hash rate in order to prevent any one pool from gaining dominant control over the network through hashing.

2) Fees: Pools charge fees from each payout that helps to support the operation of the pool. Pool fees can range from less than 1% to 4%. Depending on other factors, it makes sense to choose a pool with

lower fees in order to maximize the reward for the individual miners. Some payout models may incur higher fees in order to cover risk assumed by the pool operator; especially in cases where network rewards are not verified quickly.

3) Payout model: There are several payout models in use by mining pools. The payout model affects how rewards for individual miners are calculated.

* PPS: Pay-Per-Share (PPS) offers a flat payout based on work submitted. If there are 10 'shares' submitted to the pool, and a miner submits one, then the miner will receive 10% of the payout. Even if the single share submitted happens to be the share that wins the pool the network reward, the miner still receives the 10% portion.

* PPLNS: Pay-Per-Last-N-Shares offers a more variable payout system that is based on a miner's shares as a percentage of a larger number of shares that may precede the current block. This payout model encourages loyal users of the pool and discourages hopping on to a pool, winning a few blocks, and hopping off again. Newcomers to the pool will receive a proportionally lower reward

until they have established contributions within the last-N window of shares.

* PPS+: This model is a hybridized model of the previous two. The block reward is payed out using the PPS model, while any transaction rewards are payed out in the PPLNS model.

Can Ethereum overtake Bitcoin?

At the time of this writing, Bitcoin is priced at just over fifty thousand US dollars, while Ethereum is priced just over four thousand dollars. There are a few ways one could look at Ethereum overtaking Bitcoin.

Price per coin: Bitcoin's current price is over ten times that of Ethereum. While Ethereum will likely continue to increase in price over time, a 10x increase at this point is unlikely, and would put the Ethereum market cap at roughly four trillion US dollars, which seems unlikely.

Market capitalization: Bitcoin's market cap is roughly nine hundred twenty-two billion dollars; while Ethereum is *running* at four hundred ninety-five billion dollars. Thus, a 2x increase in the Ethereum price (and concomitant 2x in market cap) would cause Ethereum to overtake Bitcoin in terms of market cap. Ultimately, this 2x in market cap is a far more attainable and practical overtaking, especially as the utility of the Ethereum platform increases with the improvements being implemented.

Utility: Bitcoin is, very strictly, a single-coin crypto ecosystem. It lacks the programmability and tokenization capabilities that are baked into Ethereum. These Ethereum features are continuouly being improved through the Ethereum foundation. Ethereum has already been the platform of choice for dozens of valuable tokens and has enabled the new DeFi economy that is transforming cryptocurrency. DeFi has enabled financial mechanisms that previously were only available to major financial institutions, even though the process can - and is - summed up in a one or more smart contracts. From this perspective, it is highly likely that Ethereum has already overtaken Bitcoin.

Who controls Ethereum?

Ethereum's platform and network are generally controlled by the Ethereum Foundation, which supports the continued development of the network and software. Through their Ethereum Improvement Proposals (EIPs), proposals for improvements of the core software, network rewards, mining difficulties, etc., can be submitted to the foundation for review and possible implementation in the network.

The Ethereum Foundation maintains their website, https://www.ethereum.org, to provide all manner of information about Ethereum. From experts to the uninitiated curious, they provide information to get started using the Ethereum platform. The website is intended to be the complete portal to the Ethereum community, making it easy for providing information on Ethereum as it is, changes that are coming, and changes that are still under discussion. Through the Foundation, participants in the Ethereum network can stay informed and aware of how their investments, applications, and communities will work out in the future.

Who mines Ethereum?

Anyone with the appropriate hardware - Graphics Processing Units (GPUs), most commonly, can participate in the network and mine for Ethereum. Regular people who either happen to have the hardware, for instance gamers with an interest in cryptocurrency, or people who have purchased the hardware for mining purposes may mine - either individually or as part of a pool.

Conclusion

We hope you're learned about Ethereum—it truly is a valuable technology and one that continues to impact cryptocurrency and the world at large. We also urge you to continue learning on your own. There are many quality videos, books, and courses out there that can add to your knowledge about Ethereum, cryptocurrency, blockchain, and related subjects.

Sources

https://www.thestreet.com/crypto/ethereum/ethereum-is-still-missing-huge-amount-of-nodes-after-unintentional-hard-fork

https://ethereum.org/en/what-is-ethereum/

https://ethereum.org/en/learn/

https://www.investopedia.com/terms/e/ethereum.asp#:~:text=Ethereum%20is%20an%20open%2Dsource,financial%20services%2C%20and%20entertainment%20applications.&text=Ethereum%20has%20its%20own%20associated,to%20Bitcoin%20in%20market%20value.

https://etherscan.io/nodetracker

https://www.forbes.com/profile/vitalik-buterin/?sh=5cda9e9475dd

https://www.thestreet.com/crypto/ethereum/

ethereum-2-upgrade-what-you-need-to-know#:~:text=Right%20now%2C%20Ethereum%20can%20only,using%20sharding%20and%20other%20tactics.

https://www.cnbc.com/2021/08/05/ethereums-mining-cliff-moved-up-from-summer-2022-to-december-2021.html

https://markets.businessinsider.com/news/currencies/ethereum-london-hard-fork-eip-1559-vitalik-buterin-carbon-emissions-2021-8

https://www.economist.com/sites/default/files/creighton_university_kraken_case_study.pdf

https://coincodex.com/article/6326/top-5-ethereum-improvement-proposals-eips-that-became-popular/

https://www.investopedia.com/insights/digging-deeper-bull-and-bear-markets/

https://www.investopedia.com/terms/v/volu

meoftrade.asp

https://www.cnbc.com/2021/09/24/bitcoin-ethereum-sink-as-china-intensifies-crypto-crackdown.html

https://www.nasdaq.com/articles/a-beginners-guide-to-atomic-swaps-2021-08-20

https://www.investopedia.com/terms/1/51-attack.asp

https://www.finder.com/ethereum-inflation-rate

https://ethereum.org/en/developers/docs/nodes-and-clients/

https://www.fool.com/investing/2021/12/03/should-you-buy-ethereum-before-next-years-upgrade

https://www.poolwatch.io/coin/ethereum

https://www.cam.ac.uk/research/news/study-highlights-growing-significance-of-cryptocurrencies

https://en.wikipedia.org/wiki/Cardano

—

https://medium.com/metapherse/what-is-triple-halving-of-ethereum-and-what-does-it-matter-4a69af4eecb7

https://www.thestreet.com/crypto/ethereum/ethereum-2-upgrade-what-you-need-to-know

www.ingramcontent.com/pod-product-compliance
Lightning Source LLC
Chambersburg PA
CBHW071604210326
41597CB00019B/3398